Bicycle Repair Step by Step

D0572211

2003

Bicycle Repair Step by Step

How to Maintain and Repair Your Bicycle

Rob van der Plas

Van der Plas Publications, San Francisco

copyright © 2002 Rob van der Plas

Printed in the Republic of Korea

Publisher's information:
Van der Plas Publications
1282 7th Avenue
San Francisco, CA 94122
USA
http://www.vanderplas.net
E-mail: pubrel@vanderplas.net

Distributed or represented to the book trade by:
USA: Midpoint Trade Books, Kansas City, KS
UK: Chris Lloyd Sales and Marketing Services, Poole, Dorset
Canada: Hushion House Book Publishing, Toronto, ON
Australia: Tower Books, Frenchs Forest, NSW

Cover design:
Kent Lytle, Lytle Design, Alameda, CA

Photography for cover and text:
Neil van der Plas, San Rafael, CA

With special thanks to American Cyclery in San Francisco and A Bicycle Odyssey in Sausalito
for providing equipment used for text and cover photos

Publisher's Cataloging in Publication Data
Van der Plas, Rob. Bicycle Repair Step by Step: How to maintain and repair your bicycle.
1. Bicycles and bicycling — handbooks and manuals.
23.5 cm. Bibliography: p. Includes index
I. Title
II. Authorship
Library of Congress Control Number: 2002104475
ISBN 1-892495-39-2 (softcover edition); ISBN 1-892495-89-9 (electronic edition)

About the Author

Rob van der Plas is a mechanical engineer with a lifelong passion for cycling. Having grown up in the Netherlands, and having honed his cycling and mechanical skills in England, he has lived in California since 1968. During the years since then, he has always maintained his interest in the bicycle and cycling as an activity.

Since 1974, he has been writing articles explaining technical and safety aspects of the bicycle since 1974 in a variety of American, British, German, and Dutch cycling magazines, both addressing the bike trade and the general consumer markets. These articles have covered everything from riding in traffic and safe handling techniques off-road to frame construction materials and the workings of gearing, brakes, and lighting systems.

His first book appeared in 1978, and he has been writing bicycle-related books ever since, with some books being translated into other languages. His English language books include *The Penguin Bicycle Handbook* (1983), *The Mountain Bike Book* (1984), *The Bicycle Repair Book* (1985), *The Bicycle Commuting Book* (1988), *Bicycle Technology* (1991), *Mountain Bike Maintenance* (1994), *Road Bike Maintenance* (1997), *How to Fix Your Bike* (1998), and *Buying a Bike* (1999).

Since 1993, he has been actively involved in the annual International Conference of Cycling History (yes, there really is such a thing). Not only has he attended each session, he has also been responsible for editing and publishing the conference proceedings and for maintaining the conference web site (http://www.vanderplas. net/icch.htm).

In addition to his writing and publishing activities, he is still a regular cyclist himself, using his bike for everyday transportation, as well as for fitness and for touring. Of course, he maintains his bicycles himself. As one of the world's foremost experts in the field of bicycle technology, he has also frequently been called upon for consultation and expert witness opinions relating to bicycle patent infringement and personal injury cases involving the bicycle.

Table of Contents

Introduction

The modern bicycle is a remarkably enjoyable and efficient machine. If you have chosen a bike of the type that matches your use and the size that matches your physique, it will give you many years of use. However, things do wear out, they do come loose, and they do get out of adjustment — and sometimes they break.

That's why a bicycle needs maintenance and repair work. Maintenance is the work done to prevent any potential problems as much as possible before they occur, while repair is what's done to fix things if they do break down. This book covers both.

It's not a book to read from cover to cover, but more of a reference manual with some sections that are of such general importance that you should read them right away. These are chapters 1 through 4, which deal with general subjects and general maintenance, while the remaining chapters of the book are best used only as needed for specific operations.

Before you read on, I should alert you to the fact that not everybody calls the various parts of the bike, and the various tools used, by the same names. What's a transmission to one is called a geartrain to another and drivetrain to a third. What's called a wrench in the US is called a spanner or a key (depending on just what kind of wrench is meant) in Britain. This book adheres primarily to the terminology and spelling conventions common in the US, giving alternate (mainly British) terminology in parentheses only where it might otherwise not be immediately clear what is meant.

The other general comment is that this is not a cookbook. Although I have tried to offer step-by-step instructions wherever appropriate, you will be expected to look out for peculiarities of the bike you're working on. Yes, various bikes and their components have many things in common, but no, they're not identical. So you will have to make whatever adaptations it takes to apply the general instructions to your specific situation.

CHAPTER 1

Know Your Bicycle

The bicycle has evolved quite a bit in recent years. The average bike today simply works better than it did back in the early 1980s, and even relatively cheap machines can be a pleasure to ride.

Especially the performance of brakes and gears has improved vastly, while also the quality of many other parts has improved, resulting in enhanced riding pleasure.

Yet one thing applies to today's bike at least as much as it did to yesterday's: its performance drops off sharply if it is not maintained properly. Your basically great modern bike deserves careful maintenance and immediate repair if anything goes wrong. With the help of this book, that work should be easy and satisfying.

Before getting down to the actual maintenance and repair instructions, it will be a good idea to familiarize yourself with the bike and its components. You will be in a better position to evaluate and fix any problems once you know what the various parts are called, how they operate, and how they interact with one-another. That's what this chapter aims to explain, and to do so, I will "walk" you through the various functional component groups of the bike, explaining their operation along the way.

Of course, not all bikes are created equal, and some of the components may differ from one model to the next. In this book, most of the illustrations and instructions will be based on "standard" derailleur bicycles, primarily the

mountain bike and the road bike. However, there are many other bikes as well, ranging from so-called comfort bikes to recumbent bicycles and from folding bikes to tandems. Wherever the maintenance of these different machines varies significantly from that of the more common types of bikes, model-specific instructions will be provided as much as practical.

If you bought your bike new recently, it probably came with a user's manual, which often contains helpful information, both with respect to handling the bike and in regards to maintenance. Be alert for differences between your particular bike and the details described in

Fig. 1.1.
Typical mountain bike with front suspension.

Fig. 1.2.
Typical full-suspension mountain bike.

Fig. 1.3.
Typical road bike.

such a manual, though, because — like this book — it's probably not written quite so specifically that all of it applies to the particular model you're dealing with.

There may also have been pull tags and/or instruction manuals for some of the components and accessories installed. Keep all these instructions for reference when you experience problems with those specific parts.

Parts of the Bicycle

Fig. 1.4 shows a typical bicycle with the names of the various components. Although this is a mountain bike, most of the same components can be found on most other bikes as well — though sometimes in slightly different shape or mounted in a slightly different location. To ease the process of describing these many parts, I will treat them in functional groups as follows:

- frame
- wheels
- brakes
- drivetrain
- gearing system
- steering system
- saddle and seat post
- suspension
- accessories

In chapters 5 through 21, the individual maintenance and repair instructions will be treated, arranged roughly on the basis of these same functional groups.

The Frame

Together with the front fork, the frame forms the frameset. Together, they can be considered the bike's backbone — the structure to which all the

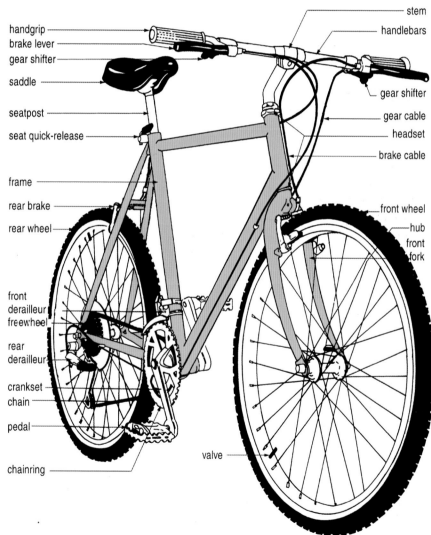

Fig. 1.4. Bike part nomenclature.

other components are attached, either directly or indirectly. Although different materials (which in turn allow for frames of different shapes) may be used on some bikes, most frames still comprise a tubular metal structure as shown in Fig. 1.11.

The front part, called main frame, is a trapezoidal structure of relatively thick tubes, called top tube, seat tube, down tube, and head tube, respectively. The rear part, referred to as rear triangle, has roughly parallel pairs of thinner tubes, called seat stays

and chain stays, respectively, that meet at the point where the rear wheel is installed.

Smaller parts are attached to the various tubes to hold other components of the bicycle: drop-outs, or fork-ends, to hold the wheels; brake bosses to hold the rear brake; seat clamp to hold the saddle; and the bottom bracket shell to hold the bearings for the cranks. The bearings for the steering system are installed in the head tube.

The frame is not really a candidate for maintenance and repair

work very often, but Chapter 19 deals with what little work may be required on the frame and the front fork.

The Wheels

After the frame, the wheels are the most critical part of the bicycle — and indeed the first bicycles, called draisines, or hobby horses, consisted of little more than a frame and a pair of wheels. Because they are also the most trouble-prone, they will be covered first in chapters 5, 6, 7, and 8.

Each wheel, shown in Fig. 1.13, consists of a hub and a network of spokes connecting it to the rim, on which the tire and the inner tube are mounted. The hub runs on ball bearings and is held in at the fork-ends at the front fork or drop-outs at the rear triangle of the frame.

The tire is inflated by means of a valve that protrudes inward through the rim. Most wheels are held in by means of a quick-release

Fig. 1.7. Nicely accessorized city bike.

Fig. 1.5. American cruiser.

Fig. 1.6. Folding bike.

Left: Fig. 1.8. Road touring tandem.

Right: Fig. 1.9. Excellent weather protection on a Dutch city bike.

mechanism, although on many simpler bikes they are still held in by means of hexagonal axle nuts.

The Brakes

Most bicycles are equipped with one form of hand-operated rim brake or another. All these stop the bike by pushing a pair of brake pads against the sides of the wheel rim. The brakes themselves are attached to the fork and the frame's rear triangle. Each brake is controlled by means of a lever mounted on the handle-bars — one on the right, usually for the rear brake, and one on the left, usually for the front brake. A flexible cable connects the lever with the brake itself. Fig. 1.13 shows a typical rim brake with matching brake lever and control cable, as used on a mountain bike.

Some bikes use brakes that act on the hub instead of on the rim. These include the disk brakes found on some mountain bikes, drum brakes found on some city bikes and (as an auxiliary brake) on some tandems, and the coaster brakes (called backpedalling brake in Britain), found on simple cruisers. The latter are installed only on the rear wheel and are operated by means of the chain when the rider pedals backward. Disk brakes may be operated either by means of cables, just like rim brakes, or by means of a hydraulic system, as on cars and motorcycles. Drum brakes are generally operated via cables. Alternately, on traditional heavy-duty roadsters, rarely seen in the US and Britain these days, the brakes — either rim or drum brakes — may be operated via rigid rods with pivoted connections. Chapters 9 and 10 cover work on rim and hub brakes, respectively.

The Drivetrain

Also known as the transmission, this is the group of components that transfers the rider's input to the rear wheel. Because the gearing system will be dealt with in a separate section, this discussion will not include the parts involved in changing gears.

Left:
Fig. 1.10.
Two different sizes of the same general type of bicycle compared at their handlebars.

Left:
Fig. 1.11.
The frame.

Right:
Fig. 1.12
Suspension fork.

Above: Fig. 1.13.
The wheel.

Below: Fig. 1.14 Brake lever and rim brake on a mountain bike.

What will be covered here are the cranks, which are held at the frame's lowest point by means of the bearings of the bottom bracket, the pedals, the chain, the chainrings (the large gear wheels attached to the right-hand crank), and the cogs, or sprockets (the smaller gear wheels attached to the rear wheel hub), as well as the freewheel mechanism built into or attached to the rear wheel hub. Chapters 11, 12, and 13 deal with the various components of the drivetrain.

The Gearing System

The vast majority of bicycles sold these days come equipped with derailleur gearing, and that's what Chapter 14 is devoted to, while Chapter 15 deals with the less common hub gearing, which is used on some city bikes.

The derailleur system achieves changes of gear ratio, needed to adapt the rider's effort and pedaling speed, to differences in terrain conditions, by moving the chain from one combination of front chainring and rear cog

to another. Selecting a bigger chainring in the front or a smaller cog in the back results in a higher gear, e.g., for fast riding on a level road; selecting a smaller chainring or a larger cog provides a lower gear, e.g., for riding uphill. The number of available gears is calculated by multiplying the number of chainrings on the front by the number of cogs in the back — usually 27 for mountain bikes and 18 for road bikes.

These "chain-derailing" operations are carried out by means of the front and rear derailleurs, respectively (the one on the front is more commonly called changer in the UK, where the rear derailleur may be referred to as "mech," short for mechanism).

The derailleurs are controlled by means of shifters, which are usually installed on the han-

dlebars, although especially on older road bikes, they may be found on the frame's down tube. On modern road bikes, these shifters are generally integrated with the brake levers, making for convenient shifting — but expensive repair or replacement if there is a problem. In all cases, the front derailleur is controlled from the left-hand shifter, while the rear derailleur is controlled from the shifter on the

Top left: Fig. 1.15. Drum-type hub brake.

Bottom left: Fig. 1.16. The drivetrain on a derailleur bike.

Bottom center: Fig. 1.17. Derailleur gearing.

Above: Fig. 1.18. The steering system on a bike with front suspension.

Below: Fig. 1.19. Hub gearing.

Fig. 1.20. Saddle and seatpost.

right. The shifters are connected with the derailleur mechanisms by means of flexible cables.

In the case of hub gearing, shown in Fig. 1.19, gear changes are achieved by means of a kind of gear box integrated in the rear wheel hub, although there is also a version that is connected with the front chainring and the cranks — mainly used on recumbent bicycles and on some downhill mountain bikes to replace the front derailleur. Hub gear systems are controlled by means of a single shifter that is generally installed on the handlebars, operating via a flexible cable. Whereas derailleur gearing usually has a large number of (slightly) different gears, hub gears are generally limited to 7 speeds (although there are some rare and expensive exceptions with even more gears). Despite the smaller number of gears, these devices typically have a range that may be quite adequate for most riding conditions short of loaded touring and out-and-out mountain bike riding.

The Steering System

The steering system is quite critical both for riding in curves and following a straight course, but also for balancing the bike. It comprises the front fork, which holds the front wheel; the handlebars; the stem, which connects these two parts; and the headset, which allow the entire system to pivot in the frame's head tube. Maintenance of handlebars, stem, and headset is covered in chapters 16 and 17, respectively, while the fork is dealt with in Chapter 19 (together with the frame) and in Chapter 20 (if it's a suspension fork).

Saddle and Seatpost

Although perhaps the least glamorous part of the bicycle, the saddle is quite important for comfort and control of the bike. The saddle is held in place in the frame's seat tube by means of a seatpost, or seat pin, which is clamped in by means of a device called binder bolt. On many mountain bikes and folding bikes, this binder bolt takes the form of a quick-release mechanism, so the saddle height is easy to adjust. Chapter 18 deals with these components.

Suspension

Many modern bikes come with some form of suspension. That may range from a simple suspension seat post to a complex system with telescoping front forks and a multi-linkage rear suspension. Although they were first widely applied to mountain bikes, they are now also penetrating the hybrid and city bike market. Chapter 20 deals with suspension-related problems.

Accessories

Although none are shown in Fig. 1.4, there is a wide range of accessories available for the bicycle. A lot of often useful items are available to attach to the bike. They range from high-tech to very simple, and from very important to trivial — which in turn depends on the circumstances of the bike's use. Such items as locks, lights and reflectors, bicycle computers, luggage racks (carriers), and fenders (mudguards) will be covered in Chapter 21.

CHAPTER 2

Know Your Tools

Bicycle maintenance and repair operations require some tools, and although it is possible to literally spend several thousand dollars on a full set of bicycle tools, you should be able to carry out most jobs with a relatively modest assortment of tools.

These include general tools, found in any good hardware store, and bicycle-specific tools, available only in bike stores. In this chapter you will find a description of the most essential

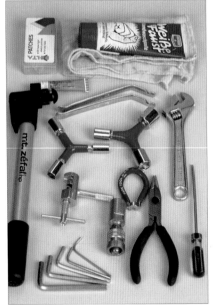

Left: Fig. 2.1. A basic tool set.

Top right: Fig. 2.2. Set of specific combination bike tools for on the road.

Bottom right: Fig. 2.3. Combination tools with Allan and socket wrenches.

tools. In the next chapter, we'll also look at the way to organize a workshop with those tools.

When buying tools, it's very important not to skimp: choose the highest quality available. Not only are good tools more accurate, they also are stronger. Although initially they'll be a lot more expensive than similar-looking "economy" tools, they'll actually turn out to be more economical in the long run because they will provide lasting service without damaging the bicycle or its components.

Equally important is to make sure tools fit accurately when selecting

tools for a particular application. Mis-matching tools may lead to serious damage of the components (and in the case of cheaper tools, also to damage of the tools themselves). Develop a feel for the fit of a tool on the matching component by trying out an adjustable wrench on a large bolt or nut. Adjust the width of the wrench's opening until it fits snugly on the flat surfaces of the bolt — no wiggling allowed here. That's the way all tools should fit the parts for which they are to be used. If they don't fit snugly, they're the wrong size.

For most general tools, I recommend buying two identical items, because in many cases you'll have to manipulate two parts of a connection at the same time to loosen, adjust, or tighten them.

Basic Tool Set

Before describing the intricacies of the many different tools for bicycle use, I suggest you buy a small selection of tools

that will serve you well for the first few jobs (and indeed for most jobs you'll ever encounter). This is also the set of tools you should carry with you on any longer bike trip (and for that purpose, you should get a pouch to hold them together that can be attached to the bike, e.g., under the saddle. Get these tools at any bike shop, where some of them will be available together in a set (in fact, you may find a set containing almost all of them together, neatly wrapped up in a pouch). Here's a list of what should be included:

- tire pump with a fitting suitable for the type of valves used on your bike's tires

- tire pressure gauge, also for the type of valves used

- set of 3 tire levers

- tire patch kit (patches, adhesive, and sandpaper or scraper)

- set of metric Allan wrenches (Allan keys) in sizes 4, 5, and 6 mm

- a flat-head and a Phillips-head screwdriver

- small adjustable wrench (spanner)

- spoke wrench (nipple spanner) to fit the spoke nipples on the wheels of your bike

- crank tools, at least the one for tightening the bolt that holds the crank to the bottom bracket axle (on new bikes often just an 8 mm Allan wrench)

- small can of spray lubricant

- cloth for cleaning

- tube of waterless hand-cleaning paste

Detailed descriptions of the individual items listed above are contained in the following sections dealing with general and bike-specific tools, respectively.

General Tools

These are the common tools (as opposed to bicycle-specific tools) that can be purchased at any general tool or hardware shop. Note though, that most bicycle components are built to metric standards, and therefore the tools will generally have to be for metric sizes, i.e., measured in mm (millimeters). This even applies to most American-made machines.

Often tools are available in the form of combination tools. Although this may be convenient for items to take with you on the bike, in general I've found individual tools more convenient to use. On the other hand, it's a good idea to buy tools in sets, because generally a set of different-sized wrenches is likely to be cheaper than it would be to buy them separately.

Many tools may have to be used in pairs (e.g., one to hold the head of a bolt, the other to hold the matching nut). Consequently, I recommend buying two tools of the same size for most of these items.

Allan wrenches

Called Allan keys in the UK, these L-shaped hexagonal rods are needed for the currently common bolts with a hexagonal recess in the head. They are identified by their across-flat dimension, corresponding to the size of the recess in which they fit. Get them in sizes from 2 mm to 10 mm to cover all possible bicycle-relevant applications.

Combination, open-ended, and box wrenches

These tools are used on hexagon-headed bolts and nuts, and other items with parallel flat exterior surfaces, primarily if you have access to

Left: Fig. 2.4. Allan wrench with matching bolt.

Right: Fig. 2.5. Combination wrench (open-ended and box wrench) with matching bolt and nut.

17

them from the side. The combination wrench is called so because it combines an open-ended wrench at one end with a box wrench (ring spanner) on the other. They are also designated by their across-flat dimension, corresponding to the dimension of the nut or bolt-head on which they fit. Get two sets in sizes from 7 mm through 17 mm. The two other types mentioned here can also be used, although they are not as convenient as their combination version.

Socket wrenches

These are also used for hexagon-headed bolts and nuts, mainly for those to which you only have access from the end (rather than the side). Usually sold in sets consisting of one or more levers or handles (often with a ratchet mechanism) and sockets with hexagon recesses in the end in several different sizes. You may need them in sizes from 7 through 17 mm.

Adjustable wrenches

This tool is similar to the open-ended wrench but is adjustable for different across-flat sizes. Most practical are the ones referred to as Crescent wrenches in the US (where that was originally a brand name). They are usually designated by their overall length, and the longer it is, the larger is also its

across-flat dimension for the bolt or the nut that it can be used on. You'll need a 6-inch and a 10-inch one. Since it's better to use non-adjustable tools, because they tend to fit more accurately, I suggest getting only one each and relying on combination wrenches and/or socket wrenches as much as possible, resorting to the adjustable wrench only when nothing else fits.

Screwdrivers

Most convenient for bicycle use are relatively short, stubby ones. Get a small, a medium, and a large one each of the regular straight-blade and the Phillips head (cross-head) variety. For bicycle use, small is

4–5 mm wide for the straight- blade screwdriver, medium is about 6–7 mm, and large is about 10 mm.

Needle-nose pliers

These tools are sometimes needed to pull a cable or a wire taut or to get hold of small items by clamping them in. If available in different sizes, get a relatively small one.

Diagonal Cutters

These tools may be needed to cut through something like a wire or a cable casing. Again, a relatively small one will probably serve you best.

Top left: Fig. 2.6. Socket wrench set.

Top right: Fig. 2.8. regular and crosshead screwdrivers with matching screws.

Bottom left: Fig. 2.7. Adjustable wrench.

Bottom right: Fig. 2.9. Diagonal cutters and needle-nose pliers.

Hammers and mallets

Yes, even for such mundane tools there's sometimes a use in bicycle mechanics. They're referenced by their weight. Get a relatively light metal-working hammer (about 300–400 g, or 10–14 oz.) and a small plastic mallet of about the same weight.

Files

Sometimes used to clean up parts with a sharp burr or items you have cut off, you'll find a use for a small half-round file, about 10 in (25 cm) long including the handle, and a similarly sized flat file, and both must be of the type designed for metal work.

Saws

This is yet another mundane item that should not be frequently used in bicycle repair. It must be designed for metal work, and I prefer the handy small one often referred to as eclipse saw.

Measuring Tools

Buy a simple measuring tape, a 30 or 45 cm metal straightedge (ruler) divided in mm, and a pair of calipers (vernier gauge), for measuring big and small items, respectively. The calipers should have both metric and inch readings, because although most of the bike's nuts and bolts are to metric standards, some other parts are made to inch sizes (e.g., the headset and the bottom bracket).

Bicycle-Specific Tools

The catalogues of bicycle tool supply companies contain literally hundreds of different tools, of which only a limited number are essential for the type of work you're likely to carry out yourself. (Many of the others are used to speed up specific jobs encountered at a bike shop but are not essential). This section contains descriptions of only the most commonly used bicycle-specific tools, all of which can be bought at most good bike shops.

Some of these tools may be specific for a particular make or model of the relevant bike component it is to be used for. The descriptions point that out wherever that may be the case. I suggest you take the bike to the shop where you buy the tools to make sure you get the appropriate version of such tools.

Repair stand

To work on the bike effectively, I highly recommend buying a work stand, to raise the bike off the ground and hold it firmly. Several different

Top left:
Fig. 2.10.
File and
small hack
saw.

Bottom left:
Fig. 2.11.
Digital and
conventional
calipers.

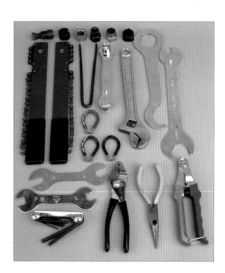

Right:
Fig. 2.12.
Set of tools,
including
bicycle-
specific
ones.

19

models are available, and I suggest you choose one that can be easily folded up and stored away when not in use.

Pump

In addition to the small pump that can be carried on the bike, you'll probably find a larger floor pump very convenient, because it allows you to inflate tires much faster and with less effort. Make sure the "head" (the fitting that goes on the valve) matches the kind of valves used on your bike, although you can buy an adaptor to switch from one type to the other. If you work on different bikes with different types of valves, it's not a bad idea to actually have a pump for each type, because it can be a hassle to switch adaptors on the pump.

Pressure gauge

This item shows the pressure to which the tires are inflated much more reliably than you can gauge it by pushing the tire in with your thumb. Although many floor pumps have one built in, I much prefer to use one that can be carried around. Make sure it matches the type of valves used on your tires.

Tire levers

These tools are used to lift the tires off the rim in order to repair or replace either the tire or the inner tube. Sold in sets of three, you should insist on thin, flat ones. Only use them for tire removal, *not* to install the tire (Chapter 8 explains how to do that correctly without using a tool).

Tire repair kit (patch kit)

This is usually sold in a little box containing adhesive patches, rubber solution (adhesive cement), and a piece of sandpaper or a scraper to roughen the area to be repaired. The little box can also be used to store other small parts.

Spoke wrench

Called nipple spanner in the UK, this tool is used to install, remove, or adjust the tension of spokes. They are available both in single units with several different-sized cutouts (for the different nipple sizes you may encounter) and as separate tools each for only one nipple size. Be very careful to choose an accurately fitting one, because you're likely to ruin the nipple if the cutout is only slightly larger than the across-flat dimension of the nipple.

Fig. 2.13. Bicycle work stand.

Top left: Fig. 2.14. Pump and pressure gauge.

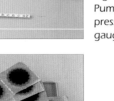

Bottom left: Fig. 2.15. Tire patch kit and tire levers.

Above: Fig. 2.16. Spoke wrenches, or nipple spanners. The green one is color-coded to a certain size nipple.

Below: Fig. 2.17. Chain tools for Hyperglide chains (left) and regular chains (right).

Chain tool

This tool is used to push one of the pins (partially) out of, and back into, the chain to allow the removal, installation, lengthening, or shortening of the chain. Some chains (specifically those marketed by Shimano under the designation Hyperglide) require a very specific version of this tool, so make sure the tool you buy matches your chain — I suggest you buy both a Hyperglide tool and a general one for all other chains.

Cone wrenches

These are thin open-ended wrenches used to

adjust, remove, or install the bearings on wheel hubs. They usually come with two different sizes on either end of the tool, and I suggest getting two each of whatever it takes to cover the size range from 13 through 17 mm.

Pedal wrench

This is a long, relatively thin, flat open-ended wrench that fits between the pedal and the crank. It has a long handle for adequate leverage to remove pedals from the crank. There are different sizes, most quality bikes requiring either 9/16 inch or 15 mm.

Crank tools

Available either as one single item combining both functions or, prefer-

ably, as two separate tools — the one a special wrench for tightening and loosening the bolt with which the cranks are attached to the bottom bracket spindle, the other an extractor for pulling the crank off the spindle. Make sure it fits the particular make and model of crank installed on your bike. You may also need a small pin wrench to remove the dust cap on the crank.

Bottom bracket tools

This may consist of either one or several special tools, depending on

the type, make, and model of the bottom bracket on your bike. Usually, though, you'll need at least a large crescent-shaped wrench with one or more prongs for the lockring and a pin wrench for the bearing cup, while the other bearing cup may require a different type of flat wrench.

Freewheel tools

These are used to remove either the screwed-on freewheel mechanism from an old-fashioned rear wheel hub with separate screwed-on freewheel or to disassemble

Top left: Fig. 2.18. Cone wrenches.
Bottom left: Fig. 2.19. Pedal wrench.

Above: Fig. 2.21. Crank tools.
Below: Fig. 2.22. Headset and cog wrenches.

Above: Fig. 2.20. Freewheel tool.

the set of cogs (sprockets) on a modern cassette-type rear hub. Get one that fits the particular freewheel or cassette used on the bikes you're going to be working on.

Chain whips and cog wrenches

These items are used in pairs for older bikes with a screwed-on freewheel (to separate the cogs), and singly for bikes with modern cassette freewheels (to restrain the freewheel when unscrewing the cog set).

Headset tools

Yet another set of thin, flat open-ended wrenches, these are designed to fit the parts of the conventional

(threaded) headset bearings. If your bike has a threaded headset (see Chapter 17), these tools will be needed for any headset adjusting and maintenance work, as well as to remove or install the front fork. They are specific to the make, model, and size of headset installed on the bike in question.

Cable cutters

Although you can cut a control cable with diagonal cutters (see *General Tools*), you'll get a cleaner cut, without frayed cable strands, by using these special cable cutters for the inner cable.

Other Tools

There are many other bicycle-specific and general tools available, which you may want to buy if the specific job you encounter requires them. Ask at a bike shop what the tools cost versus their price for fixing your problem before you invest too much in fancy tools you may rarely use.

Lubricants and Cleaners

Much maintenance of the bike consists of cleaning and lubricating the various parts. Here is a list of the items needed for that.

Bearing grease

For the ball bearings on your bike, any make of bearing grease will do the job. Get one that's available in a tube to avoid contamination of the grease due to exposure to dust and dirt.

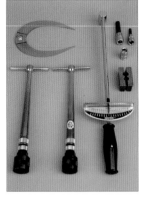

Above: Fig. 2.26. Special tools such as these are rarely needed for home bike repair work.

Below: Fig. 2.27. Lubricants and cleaning aids.

Top left: Fig. 2.23. Cassette tool for on the road.

Bottom left: Fig. 2.24. Headset tools.

Center: Fig. 2.25. Cable cutters.

Fig. 2.28. Special brush to clean the freewheel cogs.

Mineral oil

SAE 60 motor oil or any synthetic oil of similar thickness will be suitable to lubricate items that are not accessible for grease application. Even if you buy it in a can or a large bottle, put the supply you use in a small plastic squeeze bottle with a narrow spout.

Penetrating oil

Although there are special oils that are even more specifically suited to loosening overly tight connections, you will probably find that a small spray can of WD-40 does the job adequately and can be used as a lubricant in hard-to-reach places as well.

Anti-seize lubricant

A kind of paste that should be used on sensitive screw-threaded items, especially those of relatively large diameter where at least one part of the connection is made of aluminum, such as the headset, the bottom bracket, the freewheel, and the pedals.

Thread-lock compound

Most commonly known by the brand name Loctite, this is essentially an adhesive that gets applied to the type of screwed connections that might otherwise come loose too easily under the effect of vibrations when riding the bike, such as those hold-ing accessories on the bike. It's available in several different bonding strengths (in color-coded bottles), and for bike use, the one in red bottle seems to work best.

Solvents

Since solvents should be used generously and disposed of after use, I highly recommend not using terpentine or kerosene but biodegradable solvents, such as those based on citrus oil.

Wax

Both bare metal surfaces and the paint on your bike are best protected by applying wax. Any automotive wax will do the trick (don't use furniture wax).

Metal cleaner

This kind of slightly abrasive liquid or paste should be used sparingly if the bare metal of the bike's components won't return to a healthy shine any other way. Read the label to make sure it's suitable for aluminum and chrome-plated steel.

Cloths and brushes

Buy a bundle of white cleaning cloths, such as terry toweling, and two or three different-size brushes as seems appropriate for cleaning the bike and its parts. Throw out any cloths that have picked up a lot of dirt to avoid damage to the finish of bike and components, and wash out the brushes after each use.

Containers

Use a deep metal or plastic bowl, 10–12 inch (25–30 cm) in diameter, and a larger flat container for cleaning small parts and catching drips, respectively.

CHAPTER 3

Basic Maintenance Procedures

Many of the jobs to be done on the bike involve work on a small number of common parts or systems: screw threaded connections, quick-release mechanisms, cable controls, and ball bearings.

To avoid the need to explain such common principles for each repair or maintenance procedure where they apply, I have summarized them in this chapter. This way, you will be familiar with their operation, so the actual instructions in the rest of the book can be kept manageably brief.

Before we go into the instructions for dealing with the bike's individual components, here is some general advice. We'll cover four common subjects: the home workshop, spare parts, the procedures to follow when disassembling any part of the bike, and how to deal with the detailed instructions elsewhere in the book.

Equipping Your Workshop

It's nice to have a designated bike workshop but it's easy enough to improvise in a small area.

Although I now have a nicely equipped workshop in my house, I have at times set up provisional workshops in places as diverse as the corner of my bedroom and in the kitchen of a small apartment. All you need is an area of at least 7 feet (2.10 m) long and 5 feet (1.50 m) wide. By way of equipment, you will need a work stand (or some home-spun arrangement to hold the bike steady, preferably with the wheels off the ground) and a workbench. If you don't have a real workbench, a folding contraption such as a Workmate, or even an old piece of sturdily supported kitchen counter, 3 feet (90 cm) wide and 2 feet (60 cm) deep, will suffice.

Left: Fig. 3.1. A well-equipped home workshop, with tools on a board above the workbench.

Right: Fig. 3.2. The best way to work on the bike is on a work stand.

Far right: Fig. 3.3. In a pinch, you can balance the bike on a shop display stand.

As for the tools, I prefer to have them accessible on a board hung along a wall, but if you don't have room for that, you can keep them in a large tool box. If you hang them on a board on the wall, experiment with the most economic layout (placing the most frequently used tools near the bottom in the middle of the board) with the board lying flat down, then trace the tools' outlines with a bold marker, and install the hooks to hang the tools from, before installing the board on the wall. That way you'll always know which tools are missing from the board and where to hang them back.

Place items such as lubricants, solvents and cleaning materials on a shelf along one of the walls and hang some small bins (no bigger than a shoe carton) above each other for spare parts, cleaning cloths, and items to be cleaned, repaired, replaced, or discarded.

You'll need a light over the work bench and at least one over the bike. In addition, I suggest getting a drop light and putting a number of hooks in the ceiling to hang it from in different places as you may need it to shed more light on a particular part of the bike.

The bike itself is best supported on a commercially available work stand. However, bikes with flat handlebars can often be worked on by merely turning them upside-down (but turn anything mounted on the handlebars out of the way first). It is also possible to put the bike on a simple shop display stand, supporting it near the bottom bracket. Finally, you can make a simple contraption to hang the bike from the ceiling, supported at two points.

Spares and Replacement Parts

If you find any parts seriously damages or worn, they have to be replaced. For some items, you should actually have spares available. A spare tube is essential, as is a spare battery and light bulbs if you ride at night. In your home workshop, you may decide to keep a store of other minor parts as well. Just what to keep depends on how much work you find yourself doing on the bike, and only your own experience after a season's work will tell you what to keep around.

Whenever you buy spares or replacement parts, take your bike to the bike shop with you (and if you can't take the whole bike, at least take the part to be replaced and the part to which it is connected), to be sure you get something that doesn't just look like it but something that actually fits properly. For the same reason, I suggest you make a list of the make and model information for all the components installed on the bike.

I also recommend you try finding a bike shop where the owner and the mechanics are cooperative in advising you on work you want to do yourself and take the time to make sure you get the right parts and tools. Then stay with that shop as much as possible.

General Overhauling Procedures

In the course of your work on the bike and the individual components, you'll often have to remove parts or disassem-

Fig. 3.4. If you're really hard up, you can just turn the bike upside-down for some jobs. But first turn anything installed on the handlebars out of harm's way.

Right:
Fig. 3.5. On the bike work stand, clamp the bike in at a point where that does not interfere with the control cables.

ble them. If you don't go about that work systematically, you may end up with a bunch of little bits and pieces that you can't figure out how to put together again. To make your work easier, proceed as follows:

1. Select a container big enough to hold all the main parts of the item you'll be working on, and a smaller one for the small parts (on small components, you'll need only the smaller one, and a pie dish is about ideal). When taking things apart, clean and inspect each item, big or small, as you remove it and place it in the appropriate container, if at all possible, line them up in the sequence in which they were installed.

2. When disassembling a particular component, such as a brake or a pedal, it's not always necessary to remove the entire part off the bike first. Check the situation out first and decide whether it will be easier to work on it when still on the bike or

when removed in its entirety first.

- If you remove a part off the bike, first detach any controls, such as cables, then locate the main mounting bolt or bolts and remove it (or them).

- If you work with the part still on the bike, only undo those connections that would interfere with your disassembly work.

4. Work systematically, disassembling all the components in one sub-component sequence at a time and keeping all the pertinent parts together. For each item you remove, establish whether it is still in good condition and, if necessary, make a note to replace anything that appears to be seriously worn or broken.

5. When everything has been taken apart, give the components a more thorough cleaning, still keeping them together and in

sequence, as much as possible.

6. Also clean the portion of the bike where the part was installed, as well as the part(s) that you do not remove from the bike.

7. Except for parts made of natural rubber, lightly coat each component with lubricant or wax (wax for larger parts, oil for all small and hidden parts, especially those that move during operation).

8. Start reassembly working just as systematically as the disassembly process, checking for each part you assemble whether it fits properly on the other

parts already installed.

9. Once completely reassembled and installed on the bike, make any necessary hookups, such as control cables. Wipe off any excess lubricant and test the component and all its parts for proper operation. Make any adjustment necessary.

Dealing With Instructions

Wherever practical, the advice in this book is cloaked in terms of step-by-step instructions. However, usually things are not as straightforward as this method suggests. There are al-

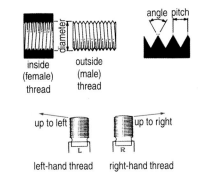

Fig. 3.6. Screw thread details.

ways variations to the way components of the bike are made and assembled; different manufacturers insert extra parts to take up extra space one way or the other; what's usually screwed on may be held in a different way on one model or another. So the message is that, although you can take these procedures as pretty good general guidelines, you should not be surprised if one or the other detail doesn't go together quite as described.

Be observant when adjusting components, checking their function and condition, and when taking them apart or reassembling them. You

Fig. 3.7. Screw thread is not only used on nuts and bolts, but also on many bearing parts, such as this conventional (threaded) headset bearing.

will usually be able to figure out between the descriptions and the actual situation as found on your bike just how the particular variant in question should be installed or operated.

If you can't figure it out yourself, take your bike to a bike shop and ask for advice there. Sometimes it will be better to have them do the work in question, especially if it requires special tools that are too expensive, considering how rarely you would need them. However, if the people at the bike shop do not encourage you to work on your bike yourself at all, I suggest you find another one with a more encouraging staff.

In addition to the instructions in this book, it will be a good idea to consult the owner's manual and/or the manuals for specific components of your bike. Especially the latter may contain useful maintenance instructions that relate specifically to the components and/or accessories installed on your particular bike.

Screw-Threaded Connections

Most of the parts on your bicycle are connected with each other by means of screwed connections. This applies not only to common nuts and bolts but also to more intricate components. The principle of screw-thread connections, simple though it seems, bears some explanation in order to manipulate them correctly. Three functions are involved: tightening, loosening, and adjusting.

All screw-threaded connections comprise a cylindrical part with a helical groove cut around the circumference (referred to as the male part, which can be e.g., a bolt or an axle) and a hollow part with a matching groove cut around the inside of the circular hole (referred to as the female part, which may be e.g., a nut).

When turning the male part relative to the female one (or vice

versa, which has the same effect), the male part enters the female one further or less far, depending on which direction it is turned. If it enters further when turning clockwise, the system has right-hand thread, which is common for all regular nuts and bolts; if it enters further when turning counterclockwise, it has left-hand thread, which is used more rarely.

Usually, there is a washer (a metal ring) between the female part and any other part that is clamped or screwed in underneath. This is to reduce the friction and make it easier to tighten and loosen the connection (thus indirectly increasing the effectiveness of the connection). Sometimes the washer takes the form of a spring washer (e.g., on minor accessories that might otherwise come loose under vibration). In other cases the washer is "keyed," which means it can only be inserted in a

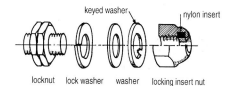

Fig. 3.8. Nut locking devices.

specific orientation (especially between screwed parts of adjustable ball bearings, to allow tightening the one part without affecting the adjustment of the other part).

To tighten a screw-thread connection, turn one of the parts clockwise relative to the other (assuming it has right-hand screw thread; counterclockwise in the case of left-hand screw thread) until it buts up against the component that is to be secured. If all is well, the resistance when turning the parts relative to each other was quite low up to this point and suddenly increases. At this stage, the two helical grooves are being pushed relative to each other and the end surfaces of the components rub against

Fig. 3.9. Use a tool each on the nut and on the bolt to tighten or loosen them relative to each other.

each other, until the force between them is so great that the connection becomes firm.

The characteristic by which screw-threaded components are identified is the outside diameter of the male part, measured in mm (millimeters) for metric components. Even though the diameter of two threaded connections may be the same, there are other aspects in which they can differ. In addition to the question of right- or left-handed thread (the latter used, e.g., on the left-hand pedal), there may be a difference in pitch (measured as the distance between consecutive grooves on the male part), and there may be a difference in the angle of the groove. The latter is not an issue for most minor items, but can matter when matching more delicate items such as crankset and headset bearing parts.

When replacing bolts and nuts, be careful to use only metric ones. In some sizes, it is hard to tell metric and Whitworth or other non-metric nuts and bolts apart (e.g., in the 5 mm size, which is deceptively similar to $3/16$ inch) and would ruin the

components due to the difference in thread pattern. The way to check if they're not marked accordingly (e.g., on the head of a bolt) is by means of a thread gauge, lining it up with the thread with the "saw-tooth" pattern of the gauge.

To loosen the connection, turn the part in the opposite direction, which at first requires force to overcome the resistance of the end surfaces, before the situation is reached where the resistance becomes much less when merely adjusting the position of the two parts relative to each other. What holds the connection in place when fastened should be the force between the helical grooves when tightened, and any other forces should be minimized to reach this force. Therefore, it is easiest to tighten (or loosen) a connection with clean and corrosion-free screw threads and end surfaces, slight lubrication, and the use of a smooth hard-surfaced washer between the end surfaces. A connection will not hold as reliably if you feel great resistance all the way due to dirt, damage, or

corrosion of threads or other surfaces.

To tighten or loosen a screwed connection, one part has to be turned in the appropriate direction with a precisely fitting tool with enough leverage, such as a wrench, while the other part must be held steady. In the case of a nut-and-bolt connection, you'll need to hold the nut with a wrench, while in the case of something screwed directly into the bicycle frame, you can hold the frame by hand or under the force of a work stand.

If you have difficulty loosening a connection that's been in place for a long time, spray some penetrating oil (e.g., WD-40) at the point where the male part engages the female, and wait 2–3 minutes before trying again.

When reinstalling screwed connections, make sure they are clean, undamaged, and not corroded — and clean, lubricate, and/or replace them with new parts if they are not. Always use a smooth washer under the head of any bolt or nut.

Regular bolts come in a variety of head shapes. These days, the

Allan head screw has become quite prevalent on bicycles, and it is indeed the most elegant, also because the hexagon recess and the matching tool seem to experience much less damage than the older flat screw cut and the hexagonal bolt head. Finally, there's the so-called grub screw (worm screw in Britain), which doesn't have a head at all — it can disappear completely into the female part. Nowadays, these usually have a (small) hexagonal recess in the end so they can be adjusted with an Allan wrench, whereas older ones are adjusted with a screwdriver.

To prevent accidental loosening of screwed connections, there are a number of different solutions. On many parts a double set of nuts is used, a thin so-called locknut and a regular nut, which are tightened against each other for a more effective hold. In fact, even a single nut may serve that same purpose if the bolt is screwed into a threaded hole of the part and then a nut is screwed on from the other side to lock it in place. In such cases (e.g., the pivot bolts on a dual-pivot brake), always disassemble by first removing the nut, then the bolt. Assemble by first screwing in the bolt until the pivot feels just right, then screw on the nut, while holding the bolt.

Nuts used on screws and bolts for accessories are often equipped with a spring washer, or lock washer, between the accessory and the nut to take up vibrating motions without loosening. More effective than the lock washer is the locking insert nut, in which a little nylon insert gets deformed around the screw thread and pushes in firmly enough to stop the nut from coming loose. Accessories should always be held with a minimum of two screws or bolts in order to minimize the effect of the unsupported mass that would cause parts to vibrate loose if held in only one spot.

When tightening (and even when loosening) threaded connections, do not apply more torque than required — to avoid damaging the head of the bolt or some other part. For this reason, choose tools of a length that's commensurate with the part in question. A 5 mm bolt or nut should not be handled with a 10-inch long adjustable wrench but with a small one (and preferably with a fixed-size — i.e., non-adjustable — wrench), which will have an appropriate length. Ideal would be to use a torque wrench on all connections, but for most components it is not so easy to find out just what amount of torque is appropriate. Choosing moderate size tools is therefore the best you can do in most cases.

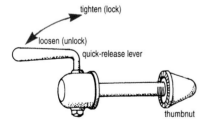

Fig. 3.10. Quick-release operation

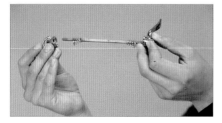

Bottom left: Fig. 3.11. On a wheel quick-release, the little conical springs go with the smaller end towards the inside.

Fig. 3.12. Quick-release in open position.

Fig. 3.13. Quick-release being put in closed position.

Especially large aluminum screw-threaded components should be handled with great care to avoid damage to the screw thread. For this reason, use only the specific tools made for these components.

When screw-threaded connections are used for adjustment, there will be one male and two female components, and the latter two are tightened against each other once the correct adjustment has been established. Since this is most commonly done in the case of adjustable ball bearings on the bike, this will be described in detail under *Ball Bearings* below.

Fig. 3.14. Quick-release on a seat clamp.

Quick-Release Mechanisms

These devices are most frequently used on the wheels to allow easy removal and installation of the wheels. The same principle of operation is also found on many brakes, in order to open them up far enough for easy wheel removal, and on the clamp that holds the seat to facilitate easy seat height adjustment. They all work on the same principle, which involves a cam-shaped device connected to a lever that can be partially rotated to tighten or loosen a connection. In most cases, the cam is hidden inside some other part, so it's hard to figure out how it works without a drawing.

When the lever is in the "open" position, the small end of the cam is engaged, leaving the connection loose. When the lever is placed in the "closed" position, the long end of the cam is

pushed just past the engagement point (the tension being at its highest when the high point of the cam was engaged), which ensures that the tension is high enough but enough force would have to be applied to move it back to the "open" position to prevent accidental opening.

If the lever is not marked with the words "open" and "close," you can still tell which is which by observing what happens when you move the lever from one position to the other. Most modern levers are shaped with a convex (bulged) surface that faces out when closed and a concave (cupped) surfaces showing when open.

In all cases, once the adjustment is correct, the secret is to operate only the lever and not the nut or other device with which the pretension of the mechanism can be adjusted, which should be left

alone whenever possible. Unfortunately, the recent trend to equip the tips of front forks of bicycles with ridges makes it impossible to use the quick-release mechanism of the hub the way it was intended. You can, of course, still loosen and tighten the mechanism properly just using the lever, but the ridge on the end of the fork blades requires you to loosen the thumb nut at the other side to provide enough play to slip over these ridges to remove or install the wheel. These ridges are being provided to prevent accidental wheel disengagement due to liability problems (that's why they're sometimes referred to as "lawyers ridges"), although when handled properly, there is no risk of accidental wheel disengagement even on forks ends without them.

Initial adjustment of the quick-release mechanism is done when the

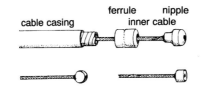

Fig. 3.15. Details of inner and outer cable.

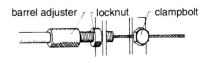

Fig. 3.16. Cable adjuster details.

bike is assembled in the factory or the bike shop, but you will probably have to do it again at some point later on after wear and tear or other factors have affected the adjustment. Proceed as follows:

Quick-release handling procedure:

1. Set the lever in the "open" position.

2. Place the device (wheel, brake, seat post) in position. If it can't be done, loosen the thumb nut at the other end far enough until things fit.

3. Place the item to be held in the exact position and orientation it should be.

4. Screw in the thumb nut until all slack is taken up, but don't forcibly tighten it.

5. Flip the lever over into the "closed" position, if possible — if it cannot be moved fully into the "closed" position, unscrew the locknut in half-turn increments until it can be closed with firm hand force.

6. Check once more whether the device is aligned properly and loosen, then re-tighten it, if necessary.

Cable Controls

Flexible cable controls are commonly used on the bicycle to operate hand brakes and gear shifting devices. They're often referred to by the name "Bowden cables" after their inventor, back in the 19th Century.

It combines a flexible stranded inner cable, or wire, to take up tension forces, with a flexible but non-compressible wound spiral outer cover, or sleeve, to take up compression forces. The ends of the outer cover are restrained in fixed cup-shaped attachments, while the inner wire has a soldered- or crimped-on nipple at one end and is clamped in at the other end.

In some cases the cables are sold only as matched sets of dimensions that are specific to a particular make and model, e.g., in the case of many modern gear-change mechanisms. Otherwise, you can just buy the outer sleeve by the foot or the meter and buy the inner cable in sections long enough to match any application (just make sure the nipple has the right shape and the cable has the same diameter as the original cable used, so it's of similar strength and flexibility).

To prevent corrosion, apply some lubricant between the inner cable and the outer sleeve. When installing a cable, run the inner cable through a wax-soaked cloth. Later, you can apply just a little oil from a spray can of lubricant at the points where the inner wire disappears into the outer sleeve whenever you do regular maintenance.

The tension of any control cable is adjusted by means of a barrel adjuster, which works in conjunction with the clamping attachment for the inner cable. Although you can usually adjust the system adequately just using this device, you may at times have to undo the clamping nut or screw and clamp the cable in at a slightly different point.

Cable adjusting procedure:

1. Check to make sure any quick-release device that may be provided in the system is

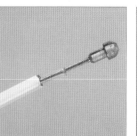

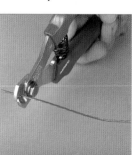

Far left: Fig. 3.17. Inner cable, sleeve, and outer cable.

Left: Fig. 3.18. Cutting an inner cable.

Right: Fig. 3.19. Outer cable with clean cut.

tensioned, and if not, tension it.

2. Verify whether it's still "out of adjustment" once the quick-release is set properly. If not, proceed to Step 3.

3. Loosen the locknut by several turns, which can usually be done by hand, without the need for a tool.

4. Turn the adjusting barrel out relative to the part into which it is screwed (to increase) or in (to reduce) the tension on the cable. Loosening will open up the brake or make the derailleur shift later;

tightening will do the opposite.

5. Holding the adjusting barrel with one hand, tighten the locknut again.

6. Check to make sure the mechanism is adjusted as intended and if not, repeat until it is.

Note:

On many newer road bikes, there is an adjuster without locknut installed on one of the brake levers or on the derailleur. In that case, instead of following steps 3 through 5, merely turn the adjuster out or in to achieve tightening or loosening, respectively.

In case of the brakes, this only works properly if you first undo the brake quick-release — and don't forget to tension it again afterwards.

If the adjustment cannot be achieved this way, the end of the cable must be clamped in at a different point — further in to tighten, out to loosen the cable.

Cable clamping procedure:

1. First release tension on the cable — either using the quick-release device, if provided, or at the barrel adjuster per steps 3 and 4 above.

2. Loosen the clamp nut or bolt that holds

the end of the cable, using a fitting tool.

3. Using needle-nose pliers, pull the cable into the appropriate position — usually no more than ¼ inch (6 mm) from its original clamping position.

4. While holding the cable in place with the pliers, tighten the clamp bolt firmly.

5. Carry out an adjustment as described above, using the barrel adjuster.

Cable friction can be minimized (improving operation of the brakes or the gears) by keeping the outer sleeve as short as possible, providing the radius of any curves in the cable is at least 10 times the diameter of the outer cable (given that most cables measure about ¼ inch, or 6 mm, they can be routed with a curve radius as tight as 2.5 inches, or 6 cm). However, you may find routing them just a little less tightly "looks" better and that's OK too — within reason.

Replace any cable that has broken strands, most typically at the end

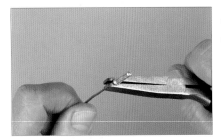

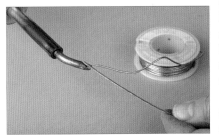

Top left: Fig. 3.19. Removing end cap from inner cable.

Bottom left: Fig. 3.20. Crimping on end cap on inner cable.

Below: Fig. 3.21. Soldering a cable to prevent fraying — hard to do on stainless steel cables.

near the nipple. If it is frayed at the other end, it may become hard to adjust, clamp in, or remove and install, so that's something to avoid.

The most common way to prevent fraying at the end is by installing a little cap over the end, which then gets crimped on. Remove it by pulling it off with pliers as shown in Fig. 3.20. To install a new cap, you must be careful the cable does not fray as you're trying to push it on. Then use pliers to crimp it on.

A better way to prevent frayed cables is to solder the strands of the cable together (you'll need a soldering iron and some rosin-core soldering wire, both readily obtainable in electronics and hardware stores). Solder the strands of the cable together before

you cut the cable, right at the spot to cut.

Ball Bearings

One of the reasons the bicycle is such an efficient vehicle is the widespread use of ball bearings. They're everywhere on the bike: wheels, pedals, cranks, headset, and freewheel mechanism. This section deals with their function and maintenance.

First off, two different types of ball bearings are in use on the bike: adjustable and non-adjustable ones, the latter usually referred to as sealed bearings. Actually, those "sealed" bearings are not really fully sealed either, and a more accurate description would be either machine bearings or cartridge bearings, the latter being the term

used elsewhere in this book.

The conventional adjustable bearing, also called cup-and-cone bearing, consists of a cup-shaped bearing race and a cone-shaped one, between which the bearing balls are contained — either loosely or held in a retainer ring — embedded in lubricant. One of the two parts (cone or cup) is adjustable by means of a screw-threaded connection, and is locked in position once it is properly adjusted by means of a lockring screwed up tightly against the screwed bearing part with an intermediate keyed washer (stopped against rotation by means of a lip or flat section that engages a groove or flat section in the male part of the threaded connection).

The advantage of the cup-and-cone bearing is that it can indeed be ad-

justed for wear. To do that, the cup and the cone are screwed closer together, which reduces the space for the bearing balls slightly, tightening the bearing. The disadvantage is that it is hard to seal such a bearing against the intrusion of dirt and water, possibly leading to wear and deterioration. For the manufacturer, the disadvantage is the fact that there are many loose parts, making assembly more difficult and costly.

The cartridge bearing has been the industry's answer to reduce assembly cost, but has been cleverly disguised as being more "high-tech" (which it isn't). It consists of pre-assembled non-adjustable components: an outer bearing race, an inner bearing race, a

Fig. 3.22. Cup-and-cone ball bearing on a wheel hub.

Fig. 3.25. Cartridge bearing on a wheel hub.

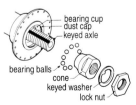

Fig. 3.23. Cup-and-cone bearing details.

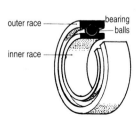

Fig. 3.24. Cartridge bearing details.

33

Fig. 3.26. Adjusting a cup-and-cone bearing.

bunch of bearing balls, held together in a retainer ring, and a set of usually neoprene (artificial rubber) seals. The disadvantage is the fact that it's not adjustable and hard to lubricate, although the advantage for the cyclist may well be less need for lubrication due to better protection against the intrusion of water and dust. When the bearing does get worn or damaged, the entire bearing assembly, the "cartridge," has to be

pulled off, requiring a special tool, and replaced, once more requiring a special matching tool.

To adjust the conventional adjustable bearing proceed as follows.

Bearing adjusting procedure:

1. Loosen the locknut at the end of the bearing assembly.

2. Lift the keyed washer clear off the cone.

3. Tu the screwed component (usually the cone, but it may be a cup-shaped part, such as on the headset) in (to tighten) or out (to loosen), after which the locknut.

4. Tighten the locknut again, while holding the cone or the bear-

ing race with another tool.

When you tighten the two screw-threaded parts against each other, the effect tends to be a slight tightening of the bearing; for that reason, the bearing should feel just a tiny bit loose before you do that. Even so, check to make sure the bearing is adjusted to run smoothly without noticeable play — and if not, tighten or loosen the parts a little and repeat the operation until it is.

Lubrication, though most efficient by means of a thick mineral oil, is usually — and less messily — done with bearing grease, which gets inserted between the bearing surfaces and in which the bearing balls are embedded. Before lubricating a bearing, though, it must be thoroughly cleaned out with solvent and a clean

cloth. Whatever you do, don't spray thin spray lubricant at ball bearings, because that is more likely to introduce surface dirt into the bearing and wash out any lubricant inside than it is to act as an effective way of lubricating the bearing.

When inspecting a ball bearing, watch out for pitted and corroded surfaces — of the bearing balls or either of the bearing races (cup and cone). Replace any parts that are damaged this way, because damaged balls would rapidly start damaging the other components as well, leading to loss of efficiency. When replacing bearing balls, always replace all of them, even if some, and not all, are visibly damaged. Whenever you take a bearing apart, clean it out thoroughly and replace the lubricant.

CHAPTER 4

Preventive Maintenance

The best way to reduce the risk of accidental damage and the need for repairs is by means of regular preventive maintenance — ranging from cleaning to lubrication and adjustment of the various components. That's the subject of this chapter.

I suggest you adhere to a three-part schedule, consisting of a quick pre-ride inspection and more extensive monthly and annual inspections, during which minor problems can be fixed before they become major problems.

Fig. 4.1. Hold pump and valve straight when inflating a tire.

Just as importantly, always be alert when riding the bike, so you notice anything that may go wrong along the way, and fix such problems at the first opportunity. For instance, if you accidentally hit a pothole hard while riding, do check the condition of tire and rim afterwards, and get them fixed if needed. And when you notice something is rattling, scraping, or rubbing as you ride, find out what the cause is and correct it right away.

Finally on this subject, where you keep the bike when you're not riding it is also important for its condition. Keep it out of the rain and direct sunlight as much as possible in a place where others can't interfere with it. If you have to keep it in a public or quasi-public place — whether that's in front of your place of work or in the back yard of an apartment building, always lock it to something fixed, using a long cable that goes through the frame and the wheels as well as a large U-lock. If possible, even place a tarp over the bike — preferably one "tailored" for a bike, wrapping it all the way around to a point close to the ground.

Pre-Ride Inspection

If you take the bike out several times on the same day, that may not be necessary each time you do, but it's a good idea to follow this procedure at least for the first ride on any day you ride the bike.

Tools and equipment:

- Usually none required except any tools

needed to make corrections.

Procedure:

1. Check the quick-releases on the wheels and on the brakes to make sure they're in the closed position. The best check is to loosen them first and then tighten them. If they feel at all loose or if they don't require firm force to tighten, they're adjusted too loose. In that case, set the lever in the "open" position, tighten the thumb nut by about one turn and tighten the lever again. Repeat, if necessary.

2. Check operation of the brakes, which must be able to block rotation of the wheels when the levers are pulled to within ¾ inch (2 cm) from the handlebars. Do this by pulling each of the levers in turn while pushing down and forward on the bike at the handlebars for the front brake, and on the

saddle when testing the rear brake. Adjust the brakes, if necessary.

3. Check to make sure the handlebars are straight and tight. To do that, straddle the front wheel, holding it tightly between your legs, and apply force to the handlebars trying to twist them in the horizontal and vertical plane. Adjust and tighten, if necessary.

4. Especially if others sometimes ride your bike too, check to make sure the saddle is at the right height for you, straight, and firmly clamped in. Adjust and tighten if not.

Fig. 4.2. Simple brake check.

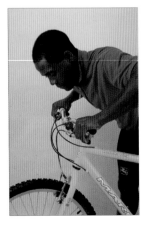

5. Check whether the tires are inflated properly — at least to the pressure listed on the sidewalls. In the beginning, always use a pressure gauge; after some practice, you'll be able to quickly feel by hand whether they're at least "about right."

6. Check operation of the gears by lifting the rear wheel off the ground and trying to engage each gear combination while turning the pedals. Adjust, if necessary.

7. Rotate both wheels, while lifted off the ground in turn, and the cranks to check whether they turn smoothly without interference, and correct, if necessary.

Monthly Inspection

The monthly inspection consists of a more thorough check and some routine maintenance operations to make up for wear, but also to take care of the cleaning and preserving that is not necessarily due to actual use of the bike but simply to the "ravages of

time." This inspection is best done in the workshop, if you have managed to arrange for one as described in Chapter 2, whereas the daily inspection is easily done almost anywhere the bike happens to be at the time.

When carrying out this (or any other) inspection, be alert to any signs of damage in addition to those specifically mentioned here. Thus, you may find some part to be loose, cracked, or otherwise damaged. Fix or replace such items as soon as you notice them. Ask for advice at a bike shop, if you're not sure whether something is serious enough to warrant replacement.

Procedure:

1. Cleaning

Clean the bike and apply protective coating as described under *Cleaning the Bike* at the end of this chapter.

2. Lubrication

Lubricate the following parts:

* The chain, spraying on a special chain spray

lubricant available at a bike shop.

* Brake levers, shifters, pivot points of exposed mechanisms and cable ends, using thin spray lubricant and aiming carefully with the thin tubular nozzle extension provided.

Afterwards, wipe off all excess lubricants to prevent parts of your bike becoming sticky and attracting dirt.

3. General check

Follow all the steps described above under *Pre-Ride Inspection*.

Fig. 4.3. Simple bottom bracket check.

4. Wheel bearings

Check the wheels for loose bearings (applying sideways force at the rim while holding the front fork for the front wheel, or the frame for the rear wheel) — if it moves, the bearings have to be adjusted as per chapters 3 and 6.

5. Wheel rim and spokes

Check the wheels for wobble and loose, bent, or broken spokes. Wheel wobble is checked by lifting the wheel off the ground and looking at it from behind at a fixed point while rotating it. If it appears to wobble sideways or up-and-down as it turns, it needs to be "trued," following

Fig. 4.4. Cleaning and polishing the paint.

the instructions in Chapter 7, which also includes instructions for dealing with loose, bent, or broken spokes.

6. Tires and tubes

Check the tires for damage and significant wear. Replace them if there are bulges, cuts, or seriously worn areas. Remove any embedded objects and replace the tube if it has been losing pressure from one day to the next. Make sure the valves are seated straight and the tires are seated equally deep all around the rims. Chapter 8 has all the relevant instructions.

7. Brakes

Check the operation of the brakes and, assuming rim brakes, observe whether the brake pads (brake blocks) touch the rim squarely over their entire length and width when you pull the brake lever to within about ¾ inch (2 cm) from the handlebars. Adjust if necessary, referring to the instructions in Chapter 9.

8. Cranks

Using either the wrench part of the crank tool or a fitting Allan wrench (depending on the crank attachment detail), tighten the bolts that hold the cranks to the bottom bracket spindle. You may have to remove a dust cap first, and reinstall it to protect the internal screw thread.

9. Accessory check

Inspect any accessories installed on the bike, as well as any you keep at home for occasional use. Make sure they are in operating order, and fix them if not. Tighten the mounting hardware for anything installed on the bike.

10. Final check

Carefully go over the entire bike and check to make sure all nuts and bolts are in place and tightened, nothing is loose, and no parts are missing or damaged. Make any corrections necessary.

Annual Inspection

This is essentially a complete overhaul, to be car-

ried out after a year's intensive use. If you ride in really bad weather and muddy terrain a lot — like real mountain biking — I'd even encourage you to carry out this inspection twice a year, once each at the end of summer and the end of winter. Proceed as follows:

Procedure:

1. Preliminary work

Clean the bike and then carry out all the work described above for the pre-ride inspection and the monthly inspection.

2. Visual Inspection

Carefully check over the entire bike and all its components and acces-

Fig. 4.5. Cleaning between cogs.

sories noting any damage, and correct anything that appears to be wrong before proceeding, following the relevant instructions in the appropriate chapters — or referring the work to a bike shop.

3. Wheels

For each wheel (still on the bike), check all around the tire and the rim for any signs of damage or serious wear, as well as bent or broken spokes, and correct anything found amiss, following the instructions in chapters 7 and 8. Then remove the wheel from the bike and overhaul the wheel hubs, referring to the instructions in Chapter 6 (if the hubs

Fig. 4.6. Cleaning in tight spots, such as here at the front derailleur.

have adjustable bearings). If the hubs have cartridge bearings, thoroughly clean the surfaces and note any signs of rough operation or looseness, in which case you should replace those bearings completely, either using a special tool or entrusting that work to a bike mechanic.

4. Chain

Remove the chain and clean it thoroughly by washing it in a container with solvent, using a brush, then letting it dry over the used solvent bath and rubbing it with a cloth. Check for apparent chain "stretch" (actually, the effect of wear). To do that, you can either use a special chain length gauge or measure the length of a 50-link section. On a new chain, that should measure 25 inches (63.7 cm), and any greater length is a sign of wear. Since 2 percent is the maximum allowable wear, replace the chain if the 50-link section measures more than 25½ inches (65 cm). Instructions for this work can be found in Chapter 13.

5. Bottom Bracket

With the cranks still attached to the bottom bracket axle, check to make sure there is no sideways play, which would indicate loose bearings. Then remove the cranks, following the instructions in Chapter 11, and spin the bottom bracket axle to make sure it rotates smoothly. If there is any sign of wear or looseness, take the bearings apart, clean and lubricate them, and adjust them (if it's an adjustable type, done from the right-hand side) or replacing the bearings (if they're of the cartridge type). Finally, reassemble the bottom bracket and the cranks, again following the instructions in Chapter 11.

6. Pedals

Turn the pedals, and check to make sure they turn freely but without play and they don't wobble as you rotate them (which would be a sign of a bent axle). If anything is not right, remove the pedals and disassemble them to clean, lubricate and adjust or replace the bearings and replace any damaged

parts, following the instructions in Chapter 12.

7. Steering

Check the operation of the headset as described above for the monthly inspection. If there is any sign of looseness or rough operation, overhaul it. See the instructions for overhauling the headset in Chapter 17.

8. Gearing

While the chain is removed for the work per Step 4 above, thoroughly clean, check, and lubricate all the components of both derailleurs (assuming derailleur gearing), making sure the pivots operate smoothly and the little wheels, or pulleys, over which the

Fig. 4.7. Cleaning around the hub bearings.

chain normally runs turn freely (unlike all other rotating parts on the bike, in their case, it's normal that they have sideways play). Fix or replace any problematic parts as explained in Chapter 14.

9. Controls

Remove the control cables for both the gearing and the brakes. Clean them, replace them if there is any damage (such as broken strands near the nipple or frayed ends on the inner cable, or kinks in the outer cable). Then rub wax onto the inner cable and reinstall the cables, referring to chapters 9 and 14 for brakes and gears, respectively.

While the cables are removed, inspect the shifter and the brake lever for smooth operation, at which time you

also have a better chance to clean and lubricate the moving parts of these devices.

After you have reinstalled the cables, check the operation of the system and make any adjustments that may be necessary, again referring to the relevant chapters 9 and 14 for brakes and gearing, respectively.

10. Accessories

If you have any accessories for the bike — whether permanently installed or not — this is the time to check their condition and operation, and take any corrective action that may be needed. Also check on any spare parts you have for the bike and/or its accessories. For example, if the spare tube you carry or keep at home has been used on the bike, make sure it is either repaired properly or

replaced by a new one. Similarly, spare bulbs or batteries for a lighting system should be checked and replaced if necessary. Finally, check the contents and condition of your tool kit and replace anything that's found wanting (e.g., the rubber solution and the patches in the tire repair kit have a limited life even if not used, and should be replaced with new ones once every two years).

Cleaning the Bike

Although it's recommended to clean your bike once a month, it may have to be done more frequently if you ride in wet and dirty terrain a lot — in fact, after every such ride. Depending on the weather and the terrain, the nature of the dirt can be quite different.

Where I live, in Northern California, we encounter about 7–8 months of dry, dusty conditions, and 4–5 months of possibly wet, muddy ones. During the wet period, it's important to avoid corrosion and thus necessary to use wax and lubricants rather generously. However, when it's dry and dusty, open lubricated parts are actually a hazard because of their tendency to hold fine dry dust particles that work like an abrasive, causing wear and rough operation of moving parts and controls.

Keep such points in mind, while otherwise generally following the following procedure.

Procedure:

1. If the bike is dry, wipe it clean as much as

Fig. 4.10. Lubricating at cable.

Left:
Fig. 4.8.
Cleaning
inside a
pedal
housing.

Right:
Fig. 4.9.
Lubricating
the front
derailleur.

Fig. 4.11. Lubricating at the rear derailleur.

possible with a soft brush or a clean cloth to remove any loose dust. If the bike is wet or the dirt is caked on, clean the bike with a bucket full of water and a sponge. Don't use a hose with a strong spray nozzle, to avoid getting water into the bearings and other sensitive parts. After washing the frame itself, take each of the other components and thoroughly clean around them.

2. Use a clean, dry cloth to dry off all the parts that got wet in the preceding operation.

3. Next, use a solvent-soaked cloth to clean the small, hidden corners of the bike and its components and accessories — from the areas around the spokes to those behind the brakes and the nooks and crannies of the derailleurs. Many of the smallest corners are best reached by wrapping the cloth around a thin, narrow object, such as a screwdriver, while the way to get between or behind the cogs and the chainrings is by folding the cloth and pulling it back-and-forth from both sides.

4. To protect the areas you've just cleaned under Step 3, do the same with a cloth soaked in lubricant or wax (use wax for dry weather, especially if it will be dusty, and oil if the weather and the terrain are more likely to be wet).

   • You can combine steps 4 and 5 by

4.12. Lubrication points.

soaking the cloth in a mixture of solvent with about 10 percent oil.

5. Treat all painted and unpainted metal surfaces of the bike and its parts with wax. If the paint or the metal surfaces appear to be weathered, you can use an automotive liquid wax that contains an abrasive compound, otherwise regular automotive wax is the material to use. Ideally, you should remove the handlebar stem and the seat post, so you can also treat the hidden portions of those parts. Reinstall them at the right height and orientation, and

make sure they're held in place firmly, following the instructions in chapters 16 and 18, respectively.

6. Rub out the wax coating with a clean, dry, soft cloth.

7. Treat all non-metallic surfaces, such as plastic (but not natural rubber, i.e., the tires), with Armor-All or a similar material for treating plastic parts of cars. Spray it on and rub it out with a clean, dry, soft cloth.

CHAPTER 5

Wheel Removal and Installation

Probably no other bicycle component requires more frequent maintenance than the wheels. This chapter provides detailed instruction for wheel removal and installation, while Chapters 6 and 7 deal with maintenance of the major components of the wheel and Chapter 8 with work on the tires.

Most wheel and tire problems require the wheel to be removed from the bicycle. Although this may seem like a mundane task, it's an important enough one to warrant the detailed instructions given below. Actually, there are quite a number of variables at play when removing a wheel, depending whether it's a front wheel or a rear wheel, whether it's held in with a quick-release or with axle nuts, and whether it's a regular wheel or one with e.g., a hub brake or hub gearing. I've lumped some of these variables together in the instructions that follow, leaving you with four categories: front and rear wheels, each with and without quick-release.

Replace Front Wheel with Quick-Release

Tools and equipment:

- Usually none required

Removal procedure:

1. Open up the brake's quick-release or ca-ble attachment to spread the brake arms apart so the tire can pass between the brake pads (assuming regular rim brakes).

- If there is no quick-release on the brake, you can either let the air out of the tire or undo the brake cable connection.

- If it should be a wheel with another type of brake, such as a disk brake or a hub brake, undo the attachment of the control cable at the brake and dislodge the counter lever — see the instructions in Chapter 10. There are even some wheels with an electric

Fig. 5.1. The wheel and its parts: hub, spokes, rim, and tire.

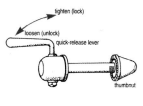

Fig. 5.2. Quick-release operation drawing.

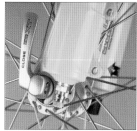

Fig. 5.3. Quick-release in "closed" position.

Fig. 5.4. Quick-release in "open" position.

generator, or dynamo, built into the hub, and on those you have to disconnect the electric wires.

2. Twist the hub quick-release lever into the "open" position.

3. If the front fork has ridges or some other component to stop the wheel, unscrew the thumbnut on the side opposite the lever until the hub can pass over them.

4. Slide the wheel out, guiding it at the hub and the rim.

Installation procedure:

1. If necessary, follow the same procedure as described in Step 1 above for wheel removal, so the wheel

will pass between the brake pads.

2. Make sure the hub's quick-release lever is in the "open" position.

3. If there are ridges on the fork ends, unscrew the thumbnut far enough for the wheel to pass over them.

4. Slide the wheel over the fork ends, guiding it near the rim between the brake pads (assuming rim brakes) until the hub is seated fully at the end of the slots in the fork ends.

5. Center the wheel at the rim between the fork blades (leaving the same distance on both sides) and tighten the quick-release lever. (In case

of ridges on the fork tips, first screw in the thumbnut until the lever can be tightened fully with significant hand force).

6. Redo any attachments and adjustments that were affected by the removal of the wheel (see Step 1 of the removal instructions above).

Replace Front Wheel with Axle Nuts

Although not much used on quality bikes these days, wheels with nutted hubs are still used (and not necessarily inferior to quick-release wheels).

Tools and equipment

- 2 wrenches to fit axle nuts

Removal procedure:

1. Open up the brake's quick-release or cable attachment to spread the brake arms apart so the tire can pass between the brake pads (assuming regular rim brakes).

  - If there is no quick-release on the brake, you can either let the air out of the tire or undo the brake cable connection.

  - If the hub has a special brake or an electric generator built in, disconnect

Fig. 5.5. Opening the quick-release.

Fig. 5.6. Closing the quick-release.

Fig. 5.7. Opening up a V-brake.

Fig. 5.8. Opening up a cantilever brake.

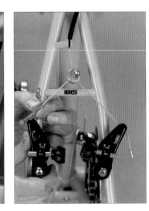

everything associated with it first.

2. Holding the axle nut on one side steady with one wrench, unscrew the one on the opposite side with the second wrench.

3. Unscrew the nuts far enough to dislodge the little plate that lies under the washer and engages in a hole in the fork blade on many front wheels with axle nuts (these serve the same purpose as the ridges on forks for use with quick-releases, namely to avoid accidental wheel disengagement).

  • If the fork blades do not have slots but round holes for

the axle nuts (sometimes the case on low-end bikes), remove the nuts and washers all the way and spread the fork blades apart by hand to remove the axle ends from those holes.

4. Slide the wheel out, guiding it at the hub and the rim.

Installation procedure:

1. If necessary, follow the same procedure as described in Step 1 above for wheel removal, so the wheel will pass between the brake pads.

2. Make sure the washer is installed and on

Fig. 5.10. Holding back the chain with the rear derailleur.

Fig. 5.9. Opening up a sidepull brake.

the outside of the fork blade, and the axle nuts are unscrewed far enough, for the little plate (if installed) to engage the matching hole in the fork blade.

3. Slide the wheel into the slots in the fork ends, guiding it near the rim between the brake pads (assuming rim brakes) until the hub is seated fully in the slots in the fork ends.

  • If the fork ends do not have slots but round holes for the axle, remove the nuts and washers all the way and spread the fork blades apart by hand to install the hub in those holes.

4. Center the wheel at the rim between the fork blades (leaving the same distance on both sides) and

Right: Fig. 5.11. Adjusting the thumbnut on a wheel quick-release.

tighten the axle nuts, tightening first the one side, then the other while holding the side that has been tightened.

6. Redo any attachments and adjustments that were affected by the removal of the wheel (see Step 1 of the removal instructions above).

Replace Rear Wheel with Quick-Release

Tools and equipment:

  • Usually only a cloth to keep your hands clean while manipulating the chain.

Removal procedure:

1. Shift the derailleurs into the gear that engages the smallest cog in the back and

the smallest chain-ring in the front.

2. Open up the brake's quick-release or cable attachment to spread the brake arms apart, so the tire can pass between the brake pads (assuming regular rim brakes).

   • If there is no quick-release on the brake, you can either let the air out of the tire or undo the brake cable connection.

   • If it should be a wheel with a disk brake or a hub brake, undo the attachment of the control cable at the brake and dislodge the counter lever — see the instructions in Chapter 10. In case it's a

wheel with a hub gear, select the highest gear and then disconnect the control for the hub gear — see Chapter 15.

3. For derailleur gearing, hold back the derailleur with the chain as shown in Fig. 5.10 to provide a straight path, unobstructed by the routing of the chain around the derailleur pulleys.

4. Twist the hub quick-release lever into the "open" position.

5. Slide the wheel out, guiding it by the hub and at the rim.

Installation procedure:

1. If applicable, follow the same procedure as described under

Step 1 above for wheel removal, so the wheel will pass between the brake pads.

2. Make sure the hub's quick-release lever is set to the "open" position.

3. Make sure the chain engages the smallest chainring in the front and the rear derailleur is set for the gear in which the chain engages the smallest cog, and route the chain over that smallest cog and around the pulleys as shown in Fig. 5.12.

4. Slide the wheel into the slot in the dropouts, guiding it near the rim between the brake pads (assuming rim brakes).

5. Let go of the chain, routing it around the smallest cog and the derailleur pulleys as shown in Fig. 5.12.

6. Center the wheel at the rim between the seat stays (leaving the same distance on both sides) and tighten the quick-release lever. (If it can't be tightened fully or if it is too loose, adjust the thumbnut until the lever can be tight-

Above: Fig. 5.14. Close-up of axle nut on a tandem rear wheel.

Below: Fig. 5.15. Loosening or tightening axle nut.

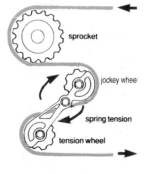

Left:
Fig. 5.12.
Chain
routing at
rear
derailleur.

Right:
Fig. 5.13.
Nutted axle
detail
drawing.

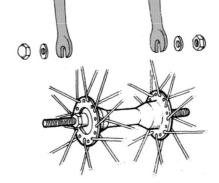

ened fully with significant hand force).

6. Redo any attachments and adjustments that were affected by the removal of the wheel (see Step 1 of the removal instructions above).

Replace Rear Wheel with Axle Nuts

Even if the bike has a quick-release on the front wheel, there may be axle nuts used in the rear.

Tools and equipment:

- 2 wrenches to fit axle nuts

- cloth to handle the chain

Fig. 5.16. Installing axle nut.

Removal procedure:

1. Open up the brake's quick-release or cable attachment to spread the brake arms apart, so the tire can pass between the brake pads (assuming rim brakes).

- If there is no quick-release on the brake, you can either let the air out of the tire or undo the brake cable connection.

- If it should be a wheel with another type of brake, such as a disk brake or a hub brake, undo the attachment of the control cable at the brake and dislodge the counter lever (see Chapter 10).

- If the bike should have hub gearing,

Fig. 5.17. The keyed plate to stop coaster brake axle from rotating goes under the axle nut washer.

select the highest gear and disconnect the control cable at the hub (see Chapter 15).

2. Holding the axle nut on one side steady with one wrench, unscrew the nut on the opposite side with the second wrench, then also loosen that nut.

3. For derailleur gearing, hold back the rear derailleur with the chain as shown in Fig. 5.10 to provide a straight path, unobstructed by the routing of the chain around the derailleur pulleys.

4. Slide the wheel out, guiding it at the hub and the rim.

Installation procedure:

1. If applicable, follow the same procedure as described in Step 1 above for wheel removal, so the wheel will pass between the brake pads (assuming regular rim brakes).

2. Make sure the washer is installed on the outside of the

dropouts and the axle nuts are unscrewed far enough to fit over the dropouts.

3. Slide the wheel into the slots in the dropouts, guiding it near the rim between the brake pads (assuming rim brakes).

4. Let go of the chain, making sure it is routed around the smallest cog and the derailleur pulleys as shown in Fig. 5.12.

5. Center the wheel at the rim between the fork blades (leaving the same distance on both sides) and tighten the axle nuts

Fig. 5.18. On this high-end non-derailleur bike, the wheel is positioned by means of eye bolts. Undo them first and reposition the wheel by screwing their nuts in just far enough.

Fig. 5.19. If there is a hub brake, undo the brake controls and the counter lever before removing the wheel, and install and readjust them during installation of the wheel.

with the wrenches, tightening first the one side, then the other while holding the side that has been tightened with one of the two wrenches.

6. Redo any attachments and adjustments that were affected by the removal of the wheel (see Step 1 of the removal instructions above).

CHAPTER 6

Wheel Hub Maintenance

This and the next two chapters deal with various aspects of wheel maintenance. Each wheel consists of a hub and a rim, with a set of spokes connecting them, and a tire with inner tube around the rim.

This chapter deals with the maintenance of the hub, while Chapter 7 covers the rim and the spokes, as well as the wheel as an overall structure. Work on the tires is covered separately in Chapter 8.

The hub consists of an axle, a set of ball bearings, and the hub body. On the sides, the hub body has flanges to accommodate the holes through which the spokes are inserted. Quick-release hubs have hollow axles, while they are solid for "bolted-on" hubs (more accurately "nutted," though that term is rarely used).

The ball bearings may be either adjustable cup-and-cone bearings or "sealed" cartridge bearings. The hub body is usually made of aluminum alloy, although it may be chrome-plated or painted steel. The number of spoke holes in the flanges must correspond to the number of spokes in the wheel, each flange usually (but not always) holding half the total number of spokes.

Hub maintenance consists of adjusting, lubricating, overhauling, or replacing the bearings, although in rare cases the axle may have to be replaced as well. All this work can be done with the wheel left assembled, whereas replacing the hub requires rebuilding the entire wheel.

Hub Bearing Check

Do this work in conjunction with the annual overhaul — and whenever you detect symptoms of wear, such as high resistance or looseness of the wheel.

Tools and equipment:

- Usually none required

Procedure:

1. First check to make sure the wheel is held into the frame or the front fork firmly, referring to the instructions in Chapter 5 to tighten it in case it is not.

2. Check whether the wheel turns freely by lifting the wheel off the ground and spinning it slowly by hand. If it

Fig. 6.1. Close-up of the hub installed in a (front) wheel.

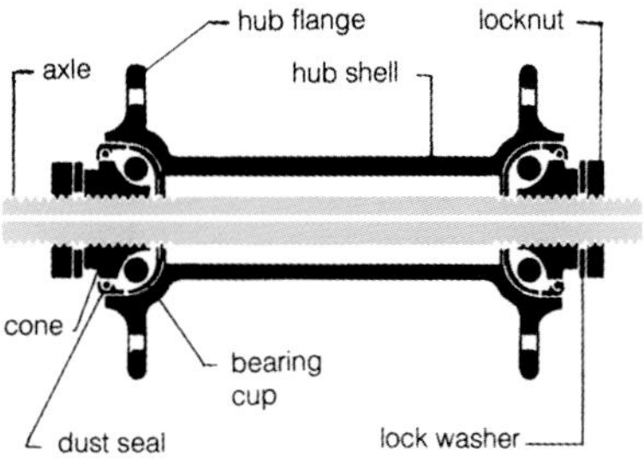

Fig. 6.2. Hub details.

Fig. 6.3. Manufacturer's illustration of a typical cassette rear hub (Shimano).

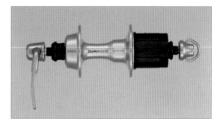

continues to rotate and sea-saws until finally coming to rest with the valve down, it's running smoothly enough. If not, the bearings must be adjusted or replaced.

3. Check whether there is play in the bearings, i.e., whether they are too loose, by holding the bike at the front fork (for the front wheel) or the frame (for the rear wheel) and trying to move the rim sideways relative to this point. If it can be moved loosely, the bearings are too loose and must be adjusted or replaced.

Hub Bearing Adjustment

This procedure only applies to hubs with cup-and-cone bearings. If the hub has cartridge bearings, refer to the instructions *Cartridge Bearing Maintenance* below.

Tools and equipment:

- cone wrenches

- open-ended wrenches or combination wrenches

Procedure:

1. Remove the wheel from the bike, as described in Chapter 5.

2. While holding the cone firmly on one side with a cone wrench, loosen the locknut on the same side by about one full turn, using either another cone wrench or a regular wrench.

3. Lift the keyed washer that's installed between the cone and the nut so it comes loose from the cone.

- If the bearing was too loose, tighten the cone about $1/8$ turn at a time, while holding the locknut on the opposite side steady with a wrench.

- If the bearing was too tight, loosen the cone about $1/8$ turn at a time, while holding the cone on the opposite side steady with another cone wrench.

5. Tighten the locknut, while holding the cone on the same side, then check the adjustment as described above and repeat the procedure, if needed, until the hub runs smoothly without sideways play. If you can't get it to run smoothly, overhaul the hub in accordance with the procedure *Hub Lubrication and Overhauling (Adjustable Bearings)* below.

6. Reinstall the wheel in the bike, following the instructions in Chapter 5.

Hub Lubrication and Overhauling (Adjustable Bearings)

This is best done in conjunction with the annual inspection summarized in Chapter 4, or whenever a bearing problem can't be solved with adjustment as described above. On a rear wheel, start on the left-hand side of the wheel because the bearing on the chain side is usually not easily accessible.

Fig. 6.4. Manufacturer's cross-section illustration of a front wheel hub (Shimano).

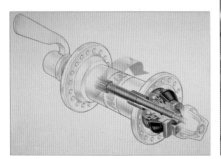

Left: Fig. 6.5. Keep the exposed area near the wheel bearings clean.

Right: Fig. 6.6. Close-up view of hub bearing.

Tools and equipment:

- cone wrenches
- open-ended or combination wrenches
- thin, flat object with leverage, e.g., narrow tire lever or wide screwdriver
- cleaning cloths
- solvent
- bearing grease

Dismantling procedure:

1. Remove the wheel from the bike and remove the quick-release or the axle nuts and washers.

2. Holding the cone on one side with one cone wrench, remove

Fig. 6.7. Adjusting the hub bearing with a cone wrench on each bearing cone.

the locknut on the same side with another cone wrench or a regular wrench.

3. Lift off and remove the lock washer, noting that it has an internal tag, or "key," that slides in a groove that runs lengthwise in the axle. Also remove any other spacers and washers that may be installed between the cone and the locknut.

4. Place the wheel horizontally (the side you're working on facing up), with a cloth under the hub. Loosen and remove the cone, holding the cone on the opposite side with a cone wrench. Catch all the bearing balls in the cloth.

5. Pull the axle out of the hub, with the cone and the locknut still installed on the opposite side, again carefully catching the

bearing balls in the cloth.

Overhauling, lubricating, and reassembly procedure:

1. Carefully pry off any plastic dust caps at the hub ends, using a thin flat object such as a tire lever (but preferably leave them in place if they are made of metal).

2. Thoroughly clean all parts — bearing balls, cones, axle, bearing races, and dust cap.

3. Inspect all parts, especially the contact surfaces of bearing races, cones, and bearing balls. Replace any parts that show signs of roughness, grooves, pitting, or corrosion.

4. Check the axle to make sure it is still straight by rolling it over a smooth level surface (e.g., a table

Left: Fig. 6.8. Lifting off the dust cap to gain access to the hub bearing.

Right: Fig. 6.9. Tightening or loosening the locknut relative to the cone.

top) — replace it if it wobbles.

5. Fill the bearing cups with bearing grease and push the bearing balls in (if you're in doubt about the correct number of balls, it should be one less than what you could squeeze in at the maximum). Then reinstall the dust caps, if they had been removed.

6. Reinsert the axle from the same side as from which it was removed, guiding it carefully so the end does not push any bearing balls out of the bearing cups.

7. Holding the end of the axle to which the cone and locknut are still attached, install the other bearing cone until almost tight — there should be just a little play left in the bearings.

Far left: Fig. 6.10. Cone removed, exposing the bearing balls.

Left: Fig. 6.11. Applying bearing grease.

Right: Fig. 6.12. Detail view of greased bearing before the cone is installed.

8. Place the keyed lock washer on the axle, aligning the key with the groove in the axle. Also install any other spacers and washers that may have been present between the cone and the locknut.

9. Install the locknut and tighten it firmly against the underlying cone.

10. Check to make sure the bearings are now adjusted to provide smooth rotation without looseness, or play — if not, adjust according to the preceding procedure *Hub Bearing Adjustment*.

11. Reinstall the wheel in the bike, following the instructions in Chapter 5.

Cartridge Bearing Maintenance

The "sealed" cartridge bearings used on many modern bikes require less maintenance because they are better protected against the intrusion of dirt, and the lubricant is better retained inside the bearings.

To replenish the lubricant, which should be done once a year, proceed as follows:

Tools and equipment:

• narrow, thin, flat screwdriver for raising the seal

• squeeze bottle or can with SAE 60 mineral oil

• cloth

• tire lever or similar flat object for pushing the seal in

Procedure:

1. Remove the wheel from the bike, following the instructions in Chapter 5.

2. Lift the neoprene seal that covers the accessible bearings up with the screwdriver.

3. While holding up the seal with the screwdriver, squirt some mineral oil past it into the bearing until it runs out the other side, catching all excess oil with the cloth, and wiping all parts clean afterwards.

4. Remove the screwdriver and push the seal back into place by hand or with the aid of a flat object, such as a tire lever.

5. To gain access to the hidden bearing inside the cassette of the rear wheel (right-hand, or chain side), the bearing on the left-hand side would have to be removed first, a job best left to a bike mechanic who has the right tools for that.

6. Also if the bearings are loose or cannot be made to operate smoothly with lubrication, they will have to be replaced by a bike mechanic using special tools.

7. Reinstall the wheel in the bike, following the instructions in Chapter 5.

CHAPTER 7

Rim and Spoke Maintenance

This chapter deals with the rim and the spokes, as well as the wheel as a complete structure. If the wheel gets damaged, it's likely to be the rim that takes the blow, and repair becomes a matter of either replacing the rim or straightening it.

Both jobs require work with the spokes — either replacing them altogether or adjusting their tension to straighten the rim.

Take a look at the way a bicycle wheel is built up. Although there are some expensive exceptions amongst lightweight and/or aerodynamic wheels intended for racing, the normal way a wheel is built up is as shown in Fig. 7.3.

Typically, there are 28, 32, or 36 spokes per wheel, half of which — every other one around the rim — run to the left-hand hub flange, the other half to the right-hand hub flange. The spokes on each side of the wheel provide radial and lateral (i.e., sideways) rigidity by pulling the rim in that direction, while the spokes on the other side pull in the opposite direction. Together, they balance the wheel both radially and laterally.

The spokes on each side of the wheel form a particular pattern (which is usually, though not always, the same on both sides). If they all run radially straight from the rim to the hub flange, it's called a radial pattern. If each spoke crosses one other spoke on the same side, it's called 1-cross; if it crosses two other spokes on the same side, it's called 2-cross, etc. Before you start work on a wheel, check the number of spokes and the spoking pattern, and if you replace any or all spokes, adhere to the same pattern. You will also need spokes of the same length (which is not necessarily the same on both sides) and thickness (referred to as "gauge").

Another thing to check before you get involved with wheel work is to check the spoke tension of a well-built new wheel. Do that by asking at a bike shop whether you can feel the spoke tension of a set of newly built wheels for a high-end bike. Check the spoke tension of the front wheel and both sides of the rear wheel

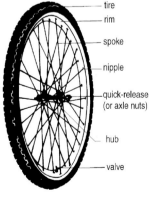

Left: Fig. 7.1. Rim and spokes of a typical (front) wheel.

Right: Fig. 7.2. There's not much you can do by way of repairs on aerodynamic bladed wheels like this one from Mavic.

Fig. 7.3. Detail drawing of spoked wheel.

tire
rim
spoke
nipple
quick-release (or axle nuts)
hub
valve

by squeezing a pair of neighboring spokes together and noticing the resistance. Then "pluck" them like musical strings and note the pitch — higher tension results in a higher pitch. When maintaining or rebuilding a wheel, aim for the same spoke tension.

Special Wheels

This chapter deals only with common spoked wheels, but there are also special aerodynamic wheels that don't use conventional wire spokes. They're usually made of carbon fiber (either completely or combined with an aluminum rim). They are hardly subject to maintenance — if bent or broken, they have to be replaced.

There are also regular, spoked, aerodynamic wheels, on which the rim has a much deeper V-section, sometimes with a special spoking pattern. These

things tend to require special spokes and nipples. It's the kind of job that should be left to a bike mechanic.

The Rim

Bicycle rims these days are almost always of one of the patterns shown in Fig. 7.4, although their depth and width may vary greatly. The inward-facing bulges at the tip of the sides serve to hook the bead of the tire into place.

The rim diameter must match the tire size — typically mountain bikes have 559 mm rims and road bikes have 622 mm rims. The width may vary from quite narrow (like 14 mm) for the lightest road racing bikes to very wide (like 32 mm) for some mountain bikes.

The number of spoke holes must match the number of spokes in the wheel and on the hub. Finally, the valve hole must be the right size

(for Presta or Schrader valves, respectively).

Wheel Truing Check

Wheel damage usually originates with a blow to the rim, deforming it either radially or laterally. When it is deformed this way, it's called "out of true," and the trick is to get it "trued" again. As a result of the deformation, some of the spokes become looser and others tighter. Often, though not always, the damaged can be repaired by selective re-tensioning of the spokes. The first thing to do is to check the extent of the damage.

Tools and Equipment:

- Usually none required, although a wheel truing stand, preferably with built-in gauges, makes the job easier.

Procedure:

1. Place the bike in the work stand or place it upside down (protecting any items mounted on the handlebars, if necessary). Or, if you do have a wheel truing stand, remove the wheel and mount it in the truing stand.

2. Slowly spin the wheel by hand and observe the distance between each side of the rim and the frame or the truing stand. Observe whether the wheel wobbles either sideways, in which case

Fig. 7.6. The rim tape (which serves to protect the inner tube) partially removed to show nipples through the rim. The "empty" hole is for the valve.

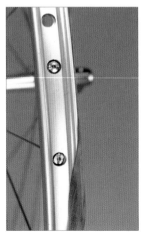

Fig. 7.4. Rim cross-section drawing.

Left:
Fig. 7.5. The parts of a conventional spoked wheel.

it's laterally out of true, or radially (apparently up-and-down as it rotates), in which case it's radially out of true. Also check whether any of the spokes are broken.

3. If there appears to be a gradual deformation over a significant area, you will probably be able to fix it by either radial or lateral truing, described below under *Wheel Truing*.

4. If there is a short, sudden deformation of the side of the rim, that is probably due to direct-impact damage of the rim, which cannot be re-

Fig. 7.7.
Adjusting the tension on a spoke by tightening the nipple with a spoke wrench.

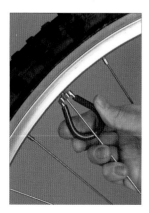

paired satisfactorily, and should be solved by replacing the entire rim, described under *Wheel Spoking/Rim Replacement* below.

5. If inspection of the wheel reveals that one or more of the spokes are broken, they must be replaced, which is described below under *Spoke Replacement*, after which the wheel has to be trued as well.

Wheel Truing

This is the work necessary to get the wheel back into shape if your wheel truing check has established that

Fig. 7.8.
Working with a truing stand.

it wobbles either sideways (i.e., it is laterally out of true) or up-and-down (i.e., it is radially out of true).

Tools and equipment:

*   spoke wrench

*   if possible, truing stand, although it can be done using the bike's frame or front fork instead for rear wheel and front wheel, respectively

*   adhesive tape or chalk for marking

*   sometimes penetrating oil and cloth

Lateral truing procedure:

1. On the basis of the wheel truing check described above, mark (e.g., with pieces of adhesive tape wrapped around the nearest spokes or chalk marks on the tire) which section of the wheel is too far to the left or the right relative to the center between the two sides of the truing stand or the frame's seat stays or front fork blades.

2. In the area thus marked, loosen the spokes that lead to the same side as to

which the buckle deviates from the center and tighten the spokes that run to the other side. Do this by turning the nipples with the spoke wrench — about one turn at the highest point of the buckle and gradually less to ¼ turn to the ones near the end of the buckled portion.

*   Which way do you turn that spoke wrench? Well, looking from the center of the wheel toward the rim, loosening is achieved when you turn clockwise, and

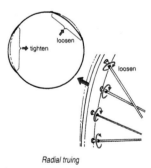

Radial truing

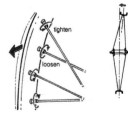

Lateral truing

Left: Fig. 7.9.
Wheel truing drawing.

tightening when you turn counterclockwise.

- If the spokes are corroded solidly in the nipples, so the nipples won't turn properly, spray some penetrating oil at the points where the spokes disappear into the nipples — and wipe off any excess — then wait 2–3 minutes before trying again.

3. Repeat Step 2 (but turning the nipples less and less as you get closer to the desired effect) until the sideways wobble is eliminated (i.e., the wheel is laterally true).

Radial truing procedure:

Using the same techniques as described in Step 1 for lateral truing, identify the "flat spot" or the "high spot" of the rim by marking the nearest

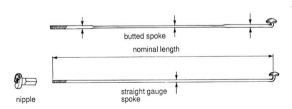

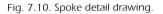

Fig. 7.10. Spoke detail drawing.

54

spokes. Then loosen the spokes in the "flat" area and tighten the ones in the "high" area until the up-and-down wobble, or "hop," is eliminated (i.e., the wheel is radially true), proceeding as in steps 2 and 3 for lateral truing above.

Emergency Buckled Wheel Repair

If the damage occurs suddenly during a ride in the form of a badly buckled ("pretzeled") wheel, e.g., as a result of hitting an obstacle, you may be able to make a provisional repair by the roadside. Ride very carefully after this, because the wheel may suddenly collapse on you if you ride too fast in corners. Once you get home, do a thorough inspection and repair, which may well mean rebuilding or replacing the entire wheel.

Tools and equipment:

- spoke wrench

Procedure:

1. Remove the wheel from the bike.

2. Find a suitable step, such as a curb stone, on which you can support one part of the rim while the other part is supported at a lower point and the hub axle stays clear of the road surface. Place the wheel in such a way that the most severe part of the outward deformation faces down on the higher support point.

3. Carefully but forcefully push down on the sections of the rim that are 90 degrees offset either side of the buckled portion. Continue or repeat until the rim is reasonably straight.

4. Place the wheel back in the bike and do a truing check as described above, then adjust the spoke tension as well as possible under the circumstances until

the wobble is minimized.

5. Ride home carefully and do a more thorough check and repair or replacement.

The Spokes

Spokes are measured in mm as shown in the illustration, i.e., from the inside of the bend to the tip of the screw-threaded end. They are available in a wide array of sizes for different combinations of hub, rim, and spoking pattern. Their thickness is also measured in mm, while the nipples must be matched with the spoke thickness and screw thread.

Fig. 7.11. This is how the spoke length is measured.

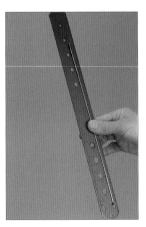

These days, most spokes are made of stainless steel. Often spokes have different thicknesses in different sections. This is referred to as "butted" meaning that the ends (butts) are thicker than the middle section — a little lighter and more flexible, reducing the chance of breakage.

Individual Spoke Replacement

This is necessary if one or more of the spokes are broken, usually at the bent portion near the head of the spoke, where it is attached to the hub flange. Replace broken spokes as soon as possible, because if you ride with one broken spoke, there is a great likelihood of additional wheel damage and more spokes breaking. Do this work with the wheel removed from the bike.

Note:

On some cheap rims, the spoke holes are not reinforced with a ferule, in which case there should be a little washer between the rim and the head of the nipple. When replacing spokes and

nipples on a rim like that, don't forget to reinstall the washers.

Tools and equipment:

- spoke wrench
- cloth and a speck of lubricant
- sometimes, tire levers and pump

Procedure:

1. Remove the remaining piece (or pieces) of the broken spoke, unscrewing the outside portion from the nipple.

2. Buy a spoke that's exactly the same length and thickness as the other spokes on the same side of the wheel.

   - If the spoke seems very loose in the nipple, you should also replace the nipple. Do that by removing a section of

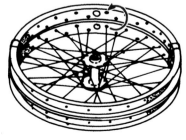

the tire and the tube as described in Chapter 8, lifting the rim tape, and prying out the old nipple. Then insert the new one and reinstall rim tape, tube, and tire.

3. Check to see how the spokes in the second hub flange hole from the spoke to be replaced run — whether the head is on the inside or the outside of the hub flange and whether it goes over or under the crossing spokes.

4. Apply a little lubricant to the threaded end of the spoke and then route the new spoke the same way as the one you observed in Step 3, screwing the nipple onto the screw-threaded end of the spoke until it has the same tension as other spokes on the same side of the wheel.

5. Check the wheel as described above under *Wheel Truing Check* and make any truing corrections as may be necessary following the description *Wheel Truing* below.

Wheel Spoking / Rim Replacement

Normally, this is a rather involved job that takes lots of practice to do effectively (or lots of time until you have lots of practice). For that reason, I recommend a simple procedure of unhooking the spokes on one rim and installing them into the new rim as you go along.

This method only works if you are replacing the rim by an identical rim (meaning you don't need spokes of different length) and you don't have to replace the spokes and the hub as well.

Fig. 7.12 (left) and 7.13 (right): Replacing identical rim by transferring spokes.

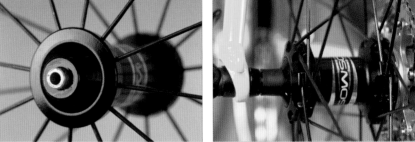

Left: Fig. 7.14. Conventional wheel with 3-cross spoking pattern.
Fig. 7.15 (center) and 7.16 (right): Different spokes: straight spokes "laced" radially in the front, tangentially in the back.

Above: Fig. 7.17. Relieving spoke stress.

Below: Fig. 7.18. Checking a wheel for centricity using a dishing tool.

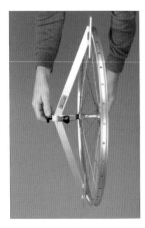

If you need to replace the spokes or the hub as well, I recommend you entrust a bike mechanic with the work instead. Before starting with this work, remove the wheel from the bike (see Chapter 5) and remove the tire and the tube from the rim (see Chapter 8).

Tools and equipment:

- spoke wrench (nipple spanner)
- if possible, truing stand, although it can be done using the bike's frame or front fork instead for rear wheel and front wheel, respectively
- adhesive tape
- lubricant and cloth
- sometimes penetrating oil

Procedure:

1. Place the new rim on top of the old one and align the valve hole of the new rim with that of the existing, while checking whether they are indeed identical in size, depth, and hole pattern.

2. Tape the two rims together in two or three spots between spoke holes.

3. Starting at the spoke next to the valve hole and working around the circumference of the wheel, undo one spoke at a time by unscrewing the nipple. Then lubricate the screw-threaded end of the spoke. Finally install the nipple in the corresponding spoke hole on the new rim and screw the nipple onto the spoke.

- If the nipples are too stiff on the spokes, apply some penetrating oil to all the spoke ends at the nipples first and wait 2–3 minutes before trying to unscrew them.

4. When all the spokes are attached to the new rim, remove the old rim and then proceed by checking the wheel for lateral and radial true and making any adjustments necessary as described under *Wheel Truing Check and Wheel Truing*, respectively, above.

Tire Maintenance

Probably no other part of the bicycle is more often in need of maintenance and repair than the tires. A puncture ("flat") is the most common mishap, but even just the frequent need for preventive maintenance — inflating them, checking for wear, and replacement of tube or tire — will always be a reminder of the drawbacks of Mr. Dunlop's great invention.

The most common type of tire is referred to as "clincher" in the US, "wired-on" in Britain. It fits around a separate inner tube and is held onto the rim by means of metal beads that are embedded in the rubber sidewalls. The sidewalls are quite flexible and the outside surface, referred to as the tread, is thicker and usually stiffer and usually has a kind of a pattern, presumably to provide more traction on a wet surface (although that's not really necessary due to the high con-tact pressure and narrow contact area between a typical bicycle tire and the road surface, which both aid in displacing water, thus preventing "aquaplaning").

The tubes are equipped with a valve to control the air pressure, and three different valve types are in use — Presta ("French"), Schrader ("auto") and Woods (a type often used in continental Europe, Asia, and Africa but rarely seen in the US and Britain). Make sure you get tubes with the same type of valve as the existing ones on your bike (they must match the valve hole in the rim, which is smaller for the Presta valve than it is for the Schrader valve). Also make sure the pump matches that type of valve, because the use of adapter nipples is very cumbersome.

Tires are designated by their nominal size, which can be given in one of several methods. In the US, the most common one reads something like 26 x 1.75, meaning the tire is approximately 26 inches in diameter and about 1¾ inches wide. More critical, though is the ETRTO designation, which is also provided, be it in small print, on the tire sidewall. It will read something like 559 x 47 (for the same tire), meaning it fits on a rim with a 559 mm diameter over the rim shoulder (where the bead of the tire is seated) and 47 mm wide. Any tire with "559" in its designation will fit this rim. For road bikes, a typical size will be something like 622 x 23, meaning it fits on a 622 mm diameter rim and is 23 mm wide

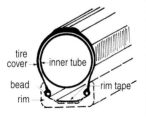

Fig. 8.1. Tire and rim cross-section drawing.

Left: Fig. 8.2. Discard a tire that's damaged this way.

Right: Fig. 8.3. Inflating a tire. Keep the valve square to the rim and the pump square to the valve.

(this particular tire is also known as 700C x 23, although it is by no means 700 mm (28 inches) in outside diameter, but closer to 668 mm, (i.e., not quite 27 inches). Just make sure you get tires that fit the rims and watch out to get a width that is small enough to clear the fork and the stays on your bike in the front and the rear, respectively.

Concerning the inner tube, other than the valve type, the size is also important, though not as critical as it is for the tire cover. Check the size range for which it is recommended before you buy one. Inner tubes have a limited shelf life (they are much more sensitive to time, heat, and humidity than the tire covers seem to be), so don't buy a large sup-

Fig. 8.4. Carry a spare tube (and the tools to do the work) on any trip.

ply of them at once, but rather buy just two at a time and replace them whenever you have to discard an existing tube due to age, number of patches, or porosity (when it starts losing air even though you can't identify a specific hole). They are available in different materials, and I like the very flexible ones made of "pure latex" (i.e., unvulcanized rubber) best — amongst other things because they are easier to patch than the ones made of butyl.

There are also different tires, called "sew-ups" in the US, "tubs" (short for "tubular tyres") in the UK. On these tires, the inner tube is encased in the outer cover, which is sewn together, giving the whole thing the appearance of a garden hose (though much more flexible). They require special rims, to which they are glued, either directly using adhesive cement or using two-sided adhesive tape, and always come with Presta valves. Since they are not used much anymore, their maintenance and repair are not covered in this book.

Tire Inflation

Well, that's what's usually said, although in reality you don't inflate the tire but the tube. Inflate the tire whenever the pressure is inadequate (anything less than the pressure marked on the sidewall is inadequate), and it's usually safe to inflate to about 30 psi, or 2 bar, more than that figure for better tire life, if you can live with the harder ride.

Tools and equipment:

- pump
- pressure gauge, if available

Procedure:

1. Make sure to use the right pump and a pressure gauge for the type of valve on the tire.

2. Check whether the valve is straight in the rim (if it isn't, let all the air out, straighten it out by manipulating the tire sidewall at the same time as the valve).

3. Remove any dust cap that may be screwed

on the end of the valve.

4. Depending on the type of valve:

   - If you're dealing with a Presta valve, unscrew the little round nut at the end and briefly push in the pin in the end to which the nut is attached to loosen it, but try not to let too much air escape.

   - If the bike has a Schrader valve, briefly push in its internal pin to loosen it, but try not to let too much air escape.

Fig. 8.5. On a Presta valve, unscrew the little round nut and push the pin in briefly to free it before pumping up the tire. Or push it in for as long as necessary to deflate the tire.

5. Check the air pressure with the pressure gauge, if available (once you have enough experience, you'll have developed a "calibrated thumb" with which you can estimate the pressure reasonably accurately without such tool).

6. Place the pump head square onto the valve, avoiding the escape of air; make sure it is seated properly on the valve and, if the pump has a toggle lever, flip the toggle lever that makes the pump head clamp around the valve more effectively.

7. Holding the pump under a right angle to the valve, inflate the tire to the desired pressure (if the pump does not have a built-in pressure gauge, check with the separate pressure gauge).

8. If the valve is of the Presta type, tighten the nut at the end, and reinstall the dust cap for either type of valve.

Inner Tube Replacement

The easiest and quickest way to "fix" a bike with a punctured tire is to replace the inner tube. However, since there's a limit to the number of inner tubes you're likely to take along, and for the sake of economy, I suggest you also learn how to actually repair a punctured tube, which will be described under *Puncture Repair* below.

Before commencing, remove the wheel from the bike, following the instructions in Chapter 5.

Tools and equipment:

- set of tire levers (preferably 3 thin flat ones)
- tire pump for the type of valve installed on the bike
- pressure gauge for the same type of valve
- spare tube of the same type and size as is installed on the bike
- preferably some talcum powder to treat the new tube so it does not deteriorate or adhere to the inside of the tire cover
- sometimes a pair of tweezers to remove sharp embedded objects from the tire cover

Procedure:

1. Remove the dust cap from the valve and let any remaining air out of the tire by pushing in the pin in the valve (after unscrewing the little round nut in the case of a Presta valve).

2. If there is a nut screwed onto the base of the valve, remove it.

3. Push the valve into the tire as far as possible to create more space for the tire bead toward the center of the rim.

4. Manipulate the tire sidewall by hand, working all around to push the bead toward the deeper center section of the rim, then work one area

Far left: Fig. 8.6. Inserting the first tire lever.

Left: Fig. 8.7. Two tire levers in place.

Right: Fig. 8.8. Removing the tire sidewall from the rim by hand.

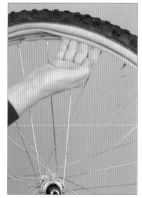

59

of the side from which you're working, some distance away from the valve, back up to the edge of the rim.

5. Place the end of the long part of the L-shaped tire lever under the tire bead over the top of the side of the rim, with the short end of the tire lever facing toward the center of the wheel. Then use it as a lever to push the bead of the tire up and over the side of the rim, hooking the notch in the short end of the lever onto a spoke.

6. Do the same with the second tire lever, about 4 spokes further to one side.

7. If necessary (i.e., if the tire sidewall can't be pushed off the rim by hand at this point), do the same with the third tire lever.

8. At this stage, you can remove the first tire lever you installed (and, if necessary, you can use it as a fourth lever, though that's rarely the case).

9. Remove the entire side of the tire cover off the rim by hand, working around gradually from the area where you used the tire levers.

10. Pull most of the inner tube out from between the tire cover and the rim.

11. Push the valve through the valve hole and remove the entire inner tube.

12. Check the condition of the tire cover inside and out, and remove any sharp embedded objects that may have been the cause of the puncture (using tweezers if you can't get them out by hand).

13. Check the condition of the rim tape that covers the deepest section of the rim bed to make sure it is intact and has the right width (it must just cover the deepest portion of the rim but not go up the sides) and no spoke ends are poking through (replace the rim tape and/or file off protruding spoke ends, as necessary).

14. Install the new tube starting at the valve, carefully making sure it is embedded properly in the deepest section of the rim under the tire.

15. Inflate the tube just a little so it is no longer "limp" but does not have noticeable pressure either.

16. Starting at the valve, pull the tire cover back over the rim, working it into the deepest section of the rim as you work your way around in both directions until it is in place over its entire circumference. The last part will probably be tough, but don't use a tire lever or any other

Fig. 8.9. Check the tire cover for damage and remove any embedded objects.

Left: Fig. 8.10. Putting the rim tape back in the center of the rim.

Below: Fig. 8.11. Putting the tube in, starting at the valve.

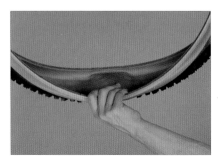

tool to do this — instead, achieve enough slack by working the bead deeper into the center section and pulling the entire tire toward the valve (you may have to let more air out of the tube), then pull the last section over from the opposite side as shown in Fig. 8.14.

17. Inflate the inner tube slightly and then "knead" the sidewalls until you're sure no part of the inner tube is caught in between the rim and the tire bead.

18. Inflate the inner tube to its final pressure, making sure the tube gets seated properly as you do so. It's seated properly if the ridge on the side is

the same distance from the rim all around the circumference on both sides, and, if necessary, correct it by first letting some air out, then "kneading" the tire, working all around until it is seated properly, and then re-inflating the tire.

19. Check the pressure with the pressure gauge and correct it, if necessary.

Puncture Repair

If you don't have (any more) spare tires with you, or once you get home, you can usually repair a damaged inner tube by patching it. Most of the work is the same as what was described above for replacing the

inner tube, so this description only covers the actual patching of the tire. To get to that stage when you have to do this by the roadside or whenever you have to repair the tube that's installed on the bike, first carry out steps 1 through 12 of the procedure *Inner Tube Replacement* above, using the tools listed there. And when you are done patching the inner tube, resume work at Step 13 of that procedure.

Tools and equipment:

- tire patch kit (adhesive patches, sand paper or abrasive scraper, rubber solution, and talcum powder)

Procedure:

1. Check the entire surface of the tube,

starting at any location you may have identified as the probable cause of the puncture on account of damage to the tire.

2. If you can't easily find the location of the leak, inflate the tube and pass it along your ear or your eye, to listen or feel where air escapes. If still no luck, dip the inflated tube in a basin with water and watch for escaping air bubbles — that's the location of the (or at least one) hole. If you have

Fig. 8.13. Pushing the tube in under the cover around the rim.

Top right: Fig. 8.14. Pulling the last part of the tire over the side of the rim by hand.

Bottom right: Fig. 8.15 Inflating the tube after installation.

Fig. 8.12. Pushing the tire sidewalls toward the (deeper) center of the rim.

dipped the tire, dry it before proceeding. Make sure you identify every leak, because there may be more than one. Mark their location by drawing a circle that's bigger than the patch you will be using around each one.

3. Rough up the area with the abrasive from the tire patch kit and wipe it clean.

4. Apply a thin, even layer of rubber solution to the area to be patched, slightly bigger than the patch you have selected, and let it dry for about 1 minute in hot weather, 2–3 minutes in cold weather — until the surface of the rubber solution becomes dull.

5. Pull one end of the protective layer (usually aluminum foil) from the patch without touching the adhesive side of the patch, and apply the patch to the treated area of the tube, centered on the hole, while pulling off the remainder of the protective layer.

6. Apply firm pressure to the entire patch for about a minute, squeezing it by hand and rubbing it e.g., with the handle of a screwdriver while supporting the tire.

7. Check to make sure the patch has adhered properly over its entire surface (and redo steps 3 through 6 if it has not).

8. Sprinkle some talcum powder over the patched area to prevent it from adhering to the inside of the tire cover. (Leaving the transparent plastic on the non-adhesive side of the patch has the same effect.)

9. Inflate the tube and wait about a minute to make sure it is not leaking, and if it is, repeat the repair for the same or any other hole you find.

10. Let the air out again and reinstall the tube under the tire cover over the rim as outlined in steps 13 through 18 of the procedure *Inner Tube Replacement* above.

Note:

Make sure the rim tape is installed properly in the middle of the rim, covering the spoke nipples, and replace it if it is damaged or missing.

Tire Cover Repair

Occasionally, you may be able to patch a tire cover if it has a small cut in it. However, it will be better to replace the tire completely if you can. If you do choose to patch it, follow the instructions above for tube repair and patch the inside cover with a small section cut from an old, thin tire. You'll have to use rubber adhesive on both the inside of the tire and on the patch. Sprinkle some talcum powder over the patch to prevent adhesion of the tire cover to the tube.

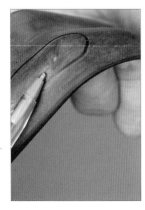

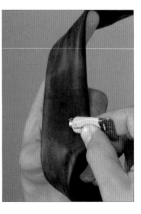

Left: Fig. 8.16. Marking the location of the hole in the tube.

Right: Fig. 8.17. Roughening the area to be treated with rubber solution (adhesive).

Far right: Fig. 8.18. Applying rubber solution to the tube.

Fig. 8.19. Spreading the rubber solution out evenly in a quick motion.

Tire Cover Replacement

When a tire cover is worn or damaged, it too has to be replaced. Make sure it has the right size, corresponding to the rim size. For mountain bike use, some tires are

Fig. 8.20. Applying the patch.

marked with a direction of rotation and sometimes there are different tires recommended for front and rear use. Pay attention to those details and make sure you get the right type and install it the right way round. (To get the direction of rotation right, visualize the tire on the bike, with the chain on the right — the top of the tire will ro-

tate forward as you look down on it.) The description is based on the wheel being removed from the bike.

Tools and equipment:

• set of 3 tire levers

• pump

• pressure gauge

• talcum powder

Procedure:

1. Treat the inside of the new tire cover with talcum powder to prevent it adhering to the inner tube.

2. Deflate the inner tube and remove the tire cover and the inner tube as described in

steps 1 through 11 of the procedure *Inner Tube Replacement*.

3. Put one side of the new tire cover over the side of the rim and push it into the center, making sure it faces the right way round if it's marked for a direction of location.

4. Put the inner tube back under the tire cover and then mount the other side of the tire cover over the rim, followed by a check and tube inflation in accordance with steps 13 through 18 of the procedure *Inner Tube Replacement* above.

CHAPTER 9

Rim Brake Maintenance

Most modern bicycles are equipped with one of two versions of the rim brake: mountain bikes usually come with so-called V-brakes, while road bikes are usually equipped with double-pivot sidepull brakes.

Other rim brakes are still around, especially on older bikes, including cantilever brakes for mountain bikes and conventional sidepull and centerpull brakes for road bikes. Hub brakes — ranging from roller brakes used on city bikes to disk brakes used on downhill mountain bikes — are making a bit of a comeback and will be covered separately in Chapter 10.

Fig. 9.1. V-brake and lever on a flat-handlebar bike.

Fig. 9.2. Double-pivot sidepull brake and lever on a road bike.

The principle of operation of all common rim brakes is that two brake pads, made of a high-friction compound and usually connected to the brake arms by means of metal holders, are pressed inward against the sides of the wheel rim. To achieve that, the rider compresses a lever that is mounted on the handlebars, which is connected to the brake mechanism by means of a flexible cable.

The V-Brake

The V-brake, also referred to as "direct-pull" or "linear-pull" brake, now commonly installed on mountain bikes and hybrids, consists of two brake arms that pivot around bosses installed directly on the fork and the seat stays. The inner and outer cable pull the upper ends of the brake arms together and the brake pads are attached to the brake arms half-way between the pivot and the cable attachment point. The inner cable is clamped directly to one brake arm, while

the outer sleeve ends in a tubular piece (referred to as "noodle") that sits in a clamp attached to the other brake arm. This is the point to undo

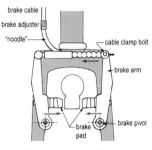

V-brake (or direct-pull brake)

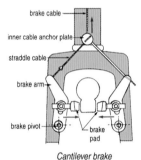

Cantilever brake

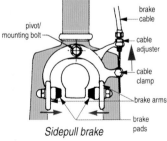

Sidepull brake

Fig. 9.3. The three most common rim brake types.

when you have to release the cable tension.

The Sidepull Brake

The sidepull brake (whether it's the now common double-pivot type or not), used on most road bikes, is a separate unit mounted by means of a single attachment bolt installed in a hole in the middle of the fork crown or the rear brake bridge (a tubular piece connecting the seat stays). Either the central bolt or two different pivots on one of the brake arms take care of the movement of the brake arms relative to each other. The brake pads are held at the lower points of the brake

arms and the inner and outer cable are attached to extensions of the two brake arms that stick out to one side. A quick-release mechanism and a cable adjuster are attached to the brake arm extension that holds the outer cable.

The Cantilever Brake

Mounted on bosses similar to the V-brake, the brake arms of the cantilever brake sticks out more to the sides. Instead of the direct attachment of the cable to the top of the brake arms, the two brake arms, which are much shorter than they are on the V-brake, are con-

nected by means of a straddle cable, which in turn is connected in the middle to the actual brake cable. The outer cable is held at a cable anchor attached to the frame some distance above the brake arms.

The Centerpull Brake

Hardly used on new bikes, it's still around on older machines. It works similarly to the cantilever brake, complete with straddle cable, but it's a separate unit, mounted the same way as the sidepull brake. The brake arms pivot around bosses that are attached to a kind of yoke, which in turn is mounted to the fork or the frame by

means of a central mounting bolt. Both sidepull and centerpull brakes are also referred to as caliper brakes.

Common Brake Features

There are a couple of aspects that all rim brakes have in common, and these are the first, and most general, points to pay attention to when checking or maintaining the brakes.

Adjustability is usually provided either at the point where the cable comes out of the lever or at the point where the cable connects to the brake mechanism. Somewhere in the system is usually a quick-release device or some easily handled method

Fig. 9.4. Used on most modern mountain and hybrid bikes: V-brake (direct-pull brake).

Fig. 9.5. Still used on tandems and touring bikes: cantilever brake.

Fig. 9.6. Most common on road bikes: dual-pivot sidepull brake, seen from the back.

Fig. 9.7. Found only on older bikes: centerpull brake.

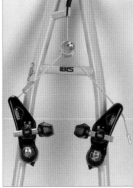
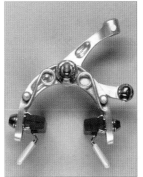

of unhooking the inner or outer cable.

The most common adjustments are those of the brake pad position relative to the rim and the cable tension. The former adjustment assures that the brake pad wears evenly and works fully when engaged; the latter adjustment determines how quickly and, indirectly, how powerfully it can be engaged.

When working on the brakes, be aware that you should be considering them as complete systems, which includes not only the brakes themselves, but also the brake levers, the control cables, and any attachments through which the cables run. In fact, even the condition of the rim and the spokes can influence brake performance.

Fig. 9.8. A rare brake: roller cam brake, mounted under the chain stays.

Brake Test

To carry out the brake test suggested for the monthly inspection — or whenever you feel the need to verify the brake's efficacy, such as before a long tour — proceed as follows:

Tools and equipment:

- Usually none required, but please wear a helmet.

Procedure:

1. Check to make sure the rims are clean, and if not, clean it with a slightly abrasive pad and water or mild solvent, followed by a dry cloth.

2. Check to make sure the brake pads are not excessively or irregularly worn, and replace them if they are.

3. Make sure the brakes themselves are firmly attached to the bike, the brake cable is firmly anchored and does not have any kinks or broken or frayed strands, and that the brake levers are firmly attached to the handlebars and can be easily reached.

4. For each brake (front and rear), check to make sure the brake pads touch the wheel rim parallel with the rim and with 1–2 mm clearance between the top of the brake pad and the edge of the rim. If not, make corrections as described under *Brake Adjustments* below.

5. Check to make sure the brake pads touch the rim firmly when you depress the

Left: Fig. 9.9. Another rare brake: U-brake, showing centering adjustment.

Right: Fig. 9.10. Conventional brake lever (without integrated brake-shifting function) for use on drop handlebars.

brake lever to within ¾ inch (2 cm) from the handlebars.

6. Get on the bike and ride it at a brisk walking speed (about 3–4 mph or 5–7 km/h) on a clear, level paved surface, such as an empty parking lot. When doing the actual test, you must be going in a straight line.

Front brake test procedure:

1. To test the front brake, apply the left-hand brake lever, gradually increasing hand force. If the bike starts to tip forward (i.e., the rear end of the bike starts lifting off the ground) once the brake is fully applied, the brake force is adequate. Immediately

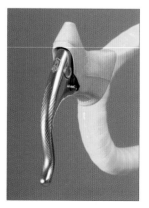

let go of the brake to prevent falling.

- If you can't get this to happen, the brake is not effective enough. Follow the procedure below to adjust the brake.

- If the bike starts to tip forward almost immediately, the brake is grabbing too vigorously for sensitively controlled braking. Follow the procedures below to adjust the brake.

- If the bike, or just the brake, vibrates, rumbles, or squeals when you apply the brake, it also needs attention as described below.

- If applying the brake seems to require excessive force at the lever, there may be a problem with either the cable or the levers, and you are referred to the relevant sections below to correct this situation.

Rear brake test procedure:

Proceed just as described above for the front brake test. However, the result will be different.

- If you can apply the brake hard enough to make the rear wheel skid while the brake lever is pulled no closer than ¾ inch (20 mm) from the handlebars, it's powerful enough.

- If you can apply the brake gradually enough to avoid skidding, you're lucky.

Brake Adjustments

The following sections contain summaries of the various procedures to improve the performance of the brake when the brake test has revealed that something's not working quite right.

Adjust Brake Application

Over time, brake pad wear, cable stretch, and pivot bushing wear in the various components combine to make the point where the brake lever activates the brake to get closer and closer to the point where the lever gets too close to the handlebars to apply sufficient force. As soon as it no longer applies powerful enough braking force

when it is ¾ inch (2 cm) from the handlebars, it must be readjusted.

Tools and equipment:

- Usually none required, sometimes wrench for cable clamp bolt at the brake.

Procedure:

1. Find the adjuster for your particular brake. On road bikes with sidepull brakes, it's usually on the brake arm to which the outer cable is anchored. On mountain bike brakes, it's usually on the brake lever at the point where the outer cable comes out of the lever body.

  - Establish what kind of adjuster it is. On

Fig. 9.12. Typical integrated brake and gear shift lever with brake applied.

Fig. 9.13. This is how brake pads should touch the rim.

Left: Fig. 9.11. Typical mountain bike brake lever.

most modern road bikes, it's the type without a locknut. On older bikes it may be the type with a locknut.

2. Also find the cable quick-release, which on most road bike brakes is on the brake arm where the inner cable is clamped in. On V-brakes, it's the bent piece of metal tubing that guides the outer cable between the brake arms — to use it, squeeze the brake arms together at the top and wiggle that tube out from the bracket that holds it at the bottom. Don't do anything yet.

3. Depending on the type of adjuster:

- If you're working on a bike with the adjuster without locknut, first use the quick-release to untension the cable. Then turn the adjuster in about one turn (to tighten) or out (in case you want the brake to grab later than it does now). Then tighten the quick-release again, check and repeat, if necessary.

- If you're working on a bike with an adjuster with a locknut (usually the case on all mountain bike brakes and on older bikes of any type), proceed as follows:

4. Loosen the locknut by several turns, which can usually be done by hand, without the need for a tool.

5. Turn the adjusting barrel relative to the part into which it is screwed (to loosen) or out (to tighten) the tension on the cable. Loosening will open up the brake; tightening will do the opposite.

6. Holding the adjusting barrel with one hand, tighten the locknut again, then check and repeat, if necessary.

7. If you run out of adjusting range, the cable has to be clamped in at a different point:

- Release the cable tension with the quick-release (or unhook the cable) and then loosen the adjuster as far as possible (after unscrewing the locknut, if present).

- Loosen the bolt or the nut that clamps the end of the inner cable at one of the brake arms (or, in the case of cantilever and centerpull brakes, the particular location where the main cable ends) by about one full turn.

- With the needle-nose pliers, pull the cable about 3/8 inch (1 cm) further in and tighten the bolt or the nut again.

Fig. 9.14.
Brake pad adjustment on mountain bike.

Fig. 9.15.
Brake pad adjustment on road bike.

Fig. 9.16. Brake cable tension adjustment on mountain bike.

8. Tighten the adjuster (and the locknut, if provided) about ¼ of the way, then tighten the quick-release and check operation of the brake — and repeat Step 6 above.

Adjust Brake Pads

Make this correction if the brake test or any other inspection revealed that the brake pads do

Above: Fig. 9.17. Brake cable tension adjustment on road bike.

Below: Fig. 9.18. Use of sidepull brake quick-release.

not lie flat and straight on the side of the rim with about ¹/₁₆ inch (1–2 mm) clearance to the tire when the brake lever is pulled in.

Tools and equipment:

• matching wrench

Procedure:

1. Holding the brake pad with one hand, undo the bolt or the nut that holds it to the brake arm by about one turn — just enough to allow controlled movement into the right position.

2. While applying the brake lever so the brake pad is pushed up against the rim, twist the brake pad into the appropriate orientation and hold

Fig. 9.19. Centering screw on dual-pivot sidepull brake.

it firmly in place there.

3. While holding the brake pad firmly, let go of the brake lever (unless you had an assistant do that for you) use the free hand to tighten the bolt or the nut that holds the brake pad to the brake arm.

4. Check to make sure both brake pads are properly aligned now and make any corrections necessary, then retighten.

Toeing in note:

Preferably, the front end (the "leading edge") of a brake pad should touch the rim first, with the whole pad settling when more force is applied. This is achieved by a procedure called "toeing in," described below under *Brake Squeal Compensation.*

Right: Fig. 9.20. Lining up the slots for removal or installation of the cable on a mountain bike brake lever.

Brake Centering

This work is required if one brake pad touches the rim before the other one, especially if it rubs on the surface of the rim while riding.

Depending on the type of brake, you may be able to find one or more small grub screws that point in vertically from the top (on a dual-pivot sidepull brake) or sideways at the pivots. Check what happens if you tighten or loosen these screws. Adjust these screws until the brake works symmetrically, if possible. Then make sure the brake is still working properly in other ways and make any final adjustments that may be needed.

If there is no such screw, or if the desired result cannot be obtained, you may have to rotate the entire brake a little (usually the case on older caliper brakes). Do

that either with a small thin wrench that fits two flat surfaces on the mounting bolt on many sidepull brakes. Otherwise, undo the mounting bolt, realign the entire brake and hold it steady there, applying force at the lever; then tighten the mounting bolt again while holding it steady.

On V- and cantilever brakes, the asymmetrical action may be due to uneven spring tension at the brake arms. To correct that, remove the brake arms, as described under *Overhaul Brake*, and either hook one or both of the springs into a different hole on the mounting plate (if provided) on the pivot boss

— or use pliers to tension one of the springs more. Then reassemble the brake arms, check operation of the brake, and make any other adjustments that may be needed.

Brake Squeal Compensation

Sometimes, brakes seem to work alright but make a squealing noise when applied. You may have to just live with it, but it's worthwhile checking whether it can be eliminated first. That's probably possible if your brake pads are mounted with some intermediate parts be-

tween the brake arm and the pad itself. These allow you to rotate the pad in another direction as well as around the mounting bolt alone (it's more common on mountain V-brakes and cantilever brakes than on road bike brakes).

If the brake pads can be rotated in the other plane, adjust the pad so that the front of the pad touches the rim when there is still 2 mm ($3/32$ inch) of "air" between the pad and the rim in the back. This condition is referred to as "toed in." If this does not do the trick, also try it the other way round, the back touching the rim first (which you might

call "toed out"). If still no luck, you'd probably best put it back in the position where the whole pad touches the rim at the same time.

Brake Rumble Compensation

If the brake rumbles, and perhaps the whole bike vibrates, when you apply the brake, it may be a matter of a irregularly dirty wheel rim, on which the brake pad does not have a good continuous contact when you apply the brake. So check that first and clean and dry the side of the rims thoroughly.

If this didn't solve the problem, it's usually because something is loose somewhere on your bike, and you'd better tighten it. First

Top left: Fig. 9.21. Replacing brake pad on a sidepull brake.

Bottom left: Fig. 9.22. Centering a sidepull brake.

Below: Fig. 9.23. Pulling in the brake lever while removing the cable on a mountain bike.

Fig. 9.24. Clamping in the cable at a V-brake.

suspect is the brake itself. Check the mounting bolts of the brakes and the individual brake arms and all related pivot points. However, sometimes it's another part of the bike that's loose — most typically the headset, for which you are referred to Chapter 17.

Replace Brake Cable

If operating the brake seems to require excessive force despite poor braking, the problem is probably due to the cable. It may be kinked, dirty, or corroded, or there may be broken strands. Inspect the cable for obvious signs of damage. Replace it if cleaning and lubrication does not alleviate the problem. Buy a replace-ment cable of at least the same length, making sure it has the same type of nipple at the end where it is hooked into the brake lever.

Tools and equipment:

- wrench for inner cable clamp bolt at brake
- needle-nose pliers
- lubricant
- cloth
- cable cutters or diagonal cutters

Procedure:

1. Undo the bolt or the nut that clamps in the cable at the brake.

2. Pull the brake lever and let go again while restraining the cable to loosen the cable. For aero-brake levers (with hidden cable), use the needle-nose pliers to grab the end of the cable near the nipple inside the brake lever, and pull enough cable free to get at it by hand to remove the rest of the inner cable. Also catch any sections of outer cable that were used and any ferrules that went around the end of the outer cable where it was held at anchor points.

- On mountain bike brake levers, the brake cable can usually be lifted out easily once you turn the adjuster and the locknut into such an orien-tation that the grooves that are cut into both parts line up with a cut-out in the brake mounting bracket.

- If there seems to be a kink in a section of outer cable that lies under the handlebar tape (that's the way the lever is configured and the upper portion of the cable is routed on most modern road bikes), remove the handlebar tape, replace that piece of outer cable and rewrap the handlebars as described in Chapter 16.

3. Apply some lubricant (wax or grease on a cloth) to the new in-

Fig. 9.26. Cutting brake cable.

Fig. 9.27. Crimping on cable end cap.

Fig. 9.28. Removing or installing V-brake arm.

Fig. 9.25. Three holes to choose from for a cantilever or V-brake.

ner cable before installing it.

4. Depress the brake lever and find the place where the cable nipple is held, then insert the cable (you may need to wiggle and twist the innards of the lever a little at the point where the nipple is held to do that).

- On mountain bike brake levers, the brake cable can usually be installed at the lever by turning the adjuster and the locknut into such an orientation that the slots cut into both parts line up with the

Fig. 9.29. Installing or removing a conventional road bike brake lever (i.e., without integrated brake-shift device).

cutout in the brake mounting bracket.

5. Route the inner cable through the various sections of outer cable and cable stops (making sure to install the ferrules at the points where the outer cable ends at the cable stops, the brake, and the lever).

6. Clamp the end of the inner cable in at the termination point on the brake while pulling it taut with the needle-nose pliers.

7. Make a provisional adjustment of the brake tension and then test the brake operation, making any final adjustments in accordance with

Fig. 9.30. Installing or removing a mountain bike brake lever.

the relevant parts of the procedure *Adjust Brake.*

Replace Brake Levers

That's probably only necessary if you've had an accident with the bike. On modern road bikes, that can be quite expensive and complex, since on these machines the brake lever is integrated with the gear shifter, making for one complex and expensive item, which affects the gearing as well. This description ignores the gearing aspect of such a job, concentrating only on the brake function of the lever. (Refer to Chapter 14 for information on work involving the gear shifting function, if that is pertinent.) Before removing the brake lever, you'll have to remove the handlebar tape and the bar-end cap on a road bike or sometimes the

Right:
Fig. 9.31. Special brake lever with a fixed "drag" position latch.

handgrip on other bike types.

Tools and equipment:

- wrench for lever mounting bolt
- needle-nose pliers
- wrench for brake cable clamp bolt (at the brake)

Procedure:

1. Remove the brake cable, following the procedure *Replace Brake Cable* above.

2. Locate the mounting bolt. If it's not externally visible, it will be accessed either from inside when you depress the brake lever (on conventional brake levers) or from under the rubber brake hood (on most integrated brake/shift levers). Loosen the bolt far enough to slide (and usually wiggle) the lever off

to the end of the handlebars.

3. Loosen the bolt on the replacement lever just far enough to allow it to slide over the handlebars (but try not to take it out all the way, because it can be very hard to get the various parts of the mounting clamp together once the bolt is out).

4. Slide the lever into position and orient it so that it can be comfortably reached while riding the bike. (If necessary, use the lever on the opposite side of the handlebars as a guide regarding the angle and the mounting position.)

5. Tighten the mounting bolt fully, making sure the lever stays in the correct position and orientation.

6. Reinstall the cable as described under *Replace Brake Cable*, and test operation of the brake, making any adjustments that may be necessary as described under *Brake Adjustments* above.

Overhaul Brake

This work differs according to the type of brake that's installed on the bike — whether it's a caliper brake (which comes off in one piece) or a mountain bike brake (on which the brake arms are mounted on pivot bosses attached to the frame or the fork).

1. Either way, first untension the quick-release or unhook the cable at the brake.

2. Depending on the type of brake:

   • If it's a V-brake or a cantilever brake, remove the brake cable clamping bolt.

   • If it's a caliper type brake, first undo the brake cable following the procedure described under *Replace Brake Cable* above, then remove the mounting bolt with which the entire brake is held to the bike.

3. Remove the bolts with which the brake arms are installed on

their pivots, then also remove the brake pads from the brake arms.

4. Remove all other components (including springs, bushings, and washers).

5. Clean and inspect the condition of all parts and replace anything damaged.

6. Slightly lubricate all parts and apply wax to the exterior surfaces, then reassemble all parts on the brake assembly (caliper brake) or the pivots (V-brake or cantilever brake).

   • On some cantilever brakes and V-brakes, there is

a choice of three holes to insert the end of the spring at each pivot, depending on the spring tension. First choose the middle hole; if after assembly the brake turns out not to be centered and no amount of adjusting will cure it, undo the brake pivot bolt again, insert the spring in one of the other holes (depending whether this was the one with too much or the one with too little tension), and reinstall the brake arm.

7. Reattach the cable and adjust it loosely, then tension the

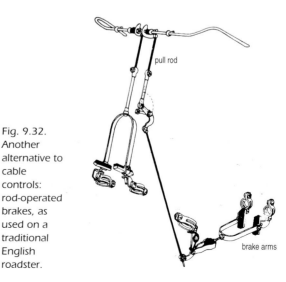

Fig. 9.32. Another alternative to cable controls: rod-operated brakes, as used on a traditional English roadster.

pull rod

brake arms

Fig. 9.33. Hydraulics can be used instead of cables. Here, it's hydraulics between the lever and the cylinder, then cable from there to the actual brake.

quick-release (caliper brake) or attach the outer cable (V-brake or cantilever brake) and make the final adjustment.

8. Test operation of the brake and make any adjustments necessary.

Hydraulic Brakes and Their Controls

Rare enough not to discuss in great detail, hydraulic brakes should at least be mentioned here. Instead of a cable, there's a hydraulic tube filled with a liquid that transfers the force from the lever (which has a cylinder and a piston to compress the liquid as the lever is depressed) to the brake. Actually, this method is more common in the case of disk brakes than it is for caliper brakes. Be careful not to pinch or otherwise damage the hydraulic tube. Occasionally, when the brake begins to feel "mushy," you should "bleed" the system (i.e., let any air bubbles out of the tube). Refer to the manufacturer's manual for this and any other maintenance details.

CHAPTER 10

Hub Brake Maintenance

rakes that operate at the center of the wheel, instead of at the rim, are referred to as hub brakes. Although still not very common, both Shimano and SRAM have in recent years introduced such brakes for use on city bikes (Shimano's version being a roller brake, SRAM's version an internal-expanding drum brake).

In addition, there are disk brakes for use on mountain bikes and a separate screwed-on drum brake (with matching special hub) for tandem use as a third brake. Then there is the band brake, common on Japanese commuter bikes. Finally there is the old standby for the American cruiser and very common in places like Holland and Germany, known as the coaster brake in the US (backpedalling brake in the UK, where it is only used on cheap children's bikes).

In this chapter you will be shown how to deal with the typical maintenance and repair work that may be required on the various kinds of hub brakes. It will not be worth your while to try and repair any of these items themselves if the instructions for adjusting and other forms of maintenance don't do the trick. If the mechanism itself fails, it will be best to take it to a bike shop and have them deal with it. (Usually the advice will be to replace the brake rather than try to fix it.)

Principle of Operation

All hub brakes have in common that friction is applied to a part connected to the wheel hub, which acts to slow the wheel down. The force is applied via a cable mechanism connected to the hand lever or (in

Fig. 10.2. Front wheel drum brake.

Fig. 10.3. Hydraulically operated disk brake.

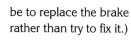

Left:
Fig. 10.1. The old standby on simple American and Northern European bikes, the coaster brake.

Right:
Fig. 10.4. Roller brake, here used in the back in combination with a seven-speed hub gear.

the case of the coaster brake) by turning the rear wheel cog back when pedaling backward. The part that is fixed and to which the brake element is attached has to be firmly anchored by means of a counter lever at some place on the frame some distance away. This counter lever also serves as the mounting point for the termination of the outer cable (except in the case of the coaster brake, of course).

In the case of the drum brake and the coaster brake, there is a set of high-friction segments inside the hub (or inside an enlarged part of the hub) that are pushed apart against the inside of the hub when

the brake is applied. In the case of the roller brake, there is a set of rollers that rise up on ramps to press against the inside of the hub. In the case of the disk brake, two brake shoes are pushed together against a round disk attached to the hub.

The band brake, finally, relies on a strap that engages the outside of a drum on the hub, and is usually controlled by means of a brake lever via a cable.

Brake Test

To check the proper operation of any of these brakes, you can follow the procedure *Brake Test* in Chapter 9, where

it was described for rim brakes. However, be prepared to encounter the following differences:

1. Roller brakes and coaster brakes are not very suitable for gradual braking. Therefore be prepared to encounter a more sudden reaction, with the brake grabbing rather vigorously at an early point in their application.

2. All these brake types, except for the disk brakes, are much more subject to overheating on long descents than rim brakes are, with the result that you can't really predict how well these brakes work when you are riding fast in hilly terrain. In fact, I'd say that, though hub brakes are perfectly suitable for most urban cycling, they should not be used for long-distance touring.

Brake Adjustment

Except for the coaster brake, all hub brakes can be adjusted by means of

an adjuster quite similar to the ones found on the various types of rim brakes. Consequently, you are referred to the relevant steps in the description *Brake Adjustments* in Chapter 9.

Brake Cable and Lever Maintenance

Also this operation will be quite similar to what was described in Chapter 9 for rim brakes, both for the cable and the lever. Refer to the relevant procedures in that chapter.

Counter Lever Problems

This lever, which is common to all hub brakes, must be firmly attached to the left-hand chainstay or fork blade (for

Fig. 10.5. Another roller brake, this one used in the front, showing the counter lever attached to the fork.

Fig. 10.6. Front drum brake showing the installation of the counter lever along the fork.

Fig. 10.7. Installing or removing the bolt that holds the counter lever, here in the back.

rear and front brake, respectively). Check its mounting bolt(s) from time to time, and tighten, if necessary.

This is also a part that will have to be loosened in order to remove the wheel — and tightened again properly upon reinstallation of the wheel. If it is not bolted directly to a welded-on plate on the frame or the fork (two bosses on the fork for a disk brake), it will be attached to a clamp that's wrapped around the left-hand chainstay or fork blade. Make sure this clamp fits

properly — if it can't be tightened properly, wrap something around the tube where the clamp goes, so that all slack is taken up. You can usually get a neoprene strip for this purpose, but if not, you can use a strip cut from an old inner tube.

There is one problem that may occur if the frame or, more typically, the front fork is not designed with a hub brake in mind. The force at the mounting point for the counter lever can be quite high, and if the fork or the frame is not de-

signed for it, it may bend or buckle at this location.

This is most typically the case if the lever is held with a clamp instead of being attached to a welded-on plate (because, if a manufacturer goes to the trouble of welding on a plate, he'll know it's intended for a hub brake and probably made it strong enough for that kind of use). So check to make sure that your hub brake is not bending the fork or the chain stays — and replace the drum brakes by regular rim brakes if the frame seems to be too light to take this kind of abuse. In fact, if there is obvious damage, you should replace the entire fork or frame, because it'll not be safe.

Hydraulic Brakes

Disk brakes, as used on some mountain bikes, are sometimes operated hydraulically instead of by means of a cable. Some models use both — a cable between the brake lever and a fixed point on the frame, and a hydraulic system from there to the brake itself.

Above: Fig. 10.11. Adjusting hub brake cable at the front brake.

Below: Fig. 10.12. Replacing brake cable.

Left: Fig. 10.8. Checking the attachment of the counter lever to make sure it's tight.

Below: Fig. 10.9. Adjusting hub brake cable at the rear brake.

Fig. 10.10. Another form of brake cable adjuster; this one needs a wrench to adjust.

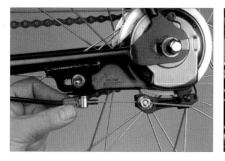

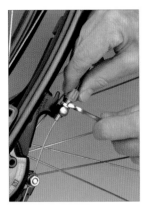

Fig. 10.13. Using a wrench to lock the adjustment into position

See the section *Hydraulic Brakes and Their Control* in Chapter 9 for relevant advice that applies to hydraulic systems in general.

Single-Speed Gearing Adaptations

Yes, even on a one-speed bike with a coaster brake or other type of hub brake, it's possible to achieve a lower or a higher gear, except, of course, you'll be stuck with that gear all the time. If you find the bike is geared too high or too low, you can replace the freewheel cog by one of a different size. To get a lower gear, replace the cog by a bigger one. For a higher gear, choose a smaller cog. For instructions, refer to Chapter 15, where this is described for the replacement of hub gear cogs.

CHAPTER 11

Crankset Maintenance

The crankset, more commonly referred to as chain-set in Britain, consists of the bottom bracket (bearings and axle), the cranks, or crank arms, and the chainrings that are connected to the left-hand crank.

The crankset is part of the bicycle's overall transmission system, also known as drivetrain — together with the pedals, the chain, and the components of the gearing system. These other items will all be covered separately in subsequent chapters.

The Cranks

Almost all modern bicycles come equipped with what is referred to as cotterless cranks — as opposed to older bikes, especially cheaper ones, on which the cranks were attached by means of cotter pins. Although you'll also be shown how to deal with the latter, we'll start off with the now common cotterless cranks. They're almost invariably made of aluminum alloy — nice and light, but it does mean that the screw thread is quite sensitive and must be treated carefully.

On these, the ends of the bottom bracket spindle are either tapered in a square pattern or splined. The crank has a correspondingly patterned recess on the inside (i.e., the side facing the bike's frame). Each crank is held on to the axle by means of a bolt (or sometimes a nut), which sits in a larger threaded cylindrical crank recess facing out. Usually there's some kind of dust cap to cover the recess. The screw thread in the cylindrical recess allows removal of the cranks with a special matching tool, although some high-end cranksets — those with splined attachments — have a clever "one-key-release" system on which the attachment bolt also serves as a crank puller (for these, you'll only require an 8 mm Allan wrench).

The right-hand crank has either a flange or, more typically, a "spider" to which the chainrings are attached at 3, 4, or 5 points by means of small bolts and nuts.

At the end opposite the one where the crank is installed on the bottom bracket axle, there is a hole with screw thread for the pedal. The one on the right has regular right-hand screw thread, while the one on the left has left-hand screw thread (that's so the left pedal doesn't work loose as you pedal the bike).

Fig. 11.1.
Typical crankset, here on a mountain bike.

Fig. 11.2.
More complicated: a tandem crankset, with chainrings on both sides.

Fig. 11.3.
Removing the crank bolt on a cotterless crankset.

Tighten Crank

Do this work in conjunction with the monthly inspection, and whenever you hear or feel creaking or other signs of looseness in the connection between the crank and the bottom bracket. Proceed as follows:

Tools and equipment:

- wrench part of crank tool or specific crank bolt wrench (for road bikes and low-end and older mountain bikes) or 8 mm Allan wrench (for modern high-end mountain bikes)

- tool to fit dust cap (depending on the model, either an Allan wrench, a pin wrench, a screwdriver, or a coin)

Procedure for bikes with large exposed Allan bolt

This type is found on most modern mountain bikes:

Fig. 11.4. Drawing of cotterless crank attachment.

1. Tighten the Allan bolt with the 8 mm Allan wrench, while holding the crank firmly for leverage.

2. Also tighten the other crank, even if it did not seem loose.

Procedure for bikes with separate metal dust cap:

1. Remove the dust cap from the threaded recess in the crank.

2. Using the wrench part of the crank tool (or a specific crank bolt wrench), tighten the bolt with the Allan wrench, while holding the crank firmly for leverage.

3. Reinstall the dust cap.

Fig. 11.5. Modern high-end cotterless crank attachment with splines instead of square axle end.

Remove and Install Crank

Do this work to gain access to the bottom bracket itself, e.g., for bearing overhaul, or to replace the crank, e.g., if it is bent or damaged.

Tools and equipment:

- crank tool (both the puller part and the crank bolt wrench part) and second wrench, or just an 8 mm Allan wrench (depending on the crank bolt type)

Procedure:

1. Remove the dust cap and then the bolt — or the Allan bolt (and the black plastic ring), or just loosen the Allan bolt (on splined-axle models, which you'll recognize by the fact that

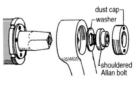

Fig. 11.6. Detail drawing showing the principle of one-key release crank attachment (shown here with regular square-tapered axle).

there is a metal cap with two little round recesses around the 8 mm Allan bolt).

- If the bolt or the nut came out (non-splined- axle models), remove any washer that may be present (very important: if you forget this step, you won't be able to pull the crank off — and ruin the screw thread in the crank).

- On splined axle models, just keep turning the bolt loose (which after the first one or two turns becomes much harder to do — but persevere anyway), and it will

Fig. 11.7. Removing the dust cap if it has two notches, using a pin wrench.

pull the crank off the axle.

3. On models requiring use of the crank extractor tool, make sure there is no washer left in the recess and the puller is fully retracted (i.e., the central threaded part does not project); then screw it into the threaded recess in the crank as far as possible, using the wrench.

4. Holding the outer part of the crank extractor tool with one wrench, screw in the central part with the other one.

5. The crank will be pulled off this way;

then unscrew the tool from the crank.

Installation Procedure:

1. Clean and inspect, and, if necessary replace parts; then apply a thin layer of grease (or preferably anti-seize lubricant) on the matching flat or splined surfaces of the bottom bracket spindle and the crank.

2. Place the crank on the bottom bracket axle, making sure it's 180 degrees offset from the other crank, and push it on by hand as far as possible.

3. On non-splined-axle models, install the

washer, then the bolt, and tighten the bolt firmly, using the crank for leverage.

4. Tighten the bolt and then, only on non-splined-axle models, install the dust cap or the plastic ring.

5. After an hour's cycling, re-tighten the bolt; and once more after another 4 hours' use — and immediately anytime it seems to be getting loose (e.g., if you hear creaking sounds).

One-key crank attachment note:

• If what looks like a dust cap around an

8 mm Allen bolt has two round recesses, it's probably the splined variety with a one-key release. On these, loosening the Allan bolt far enough actually pushes the crank off. Don't remove that thing that looks like a dust cap (you'd use a pin wrench to do so) because it is actually a restraint against which the crank bolt pushes to remove the crank, and you would have a hard time removing the crank if it were gone.

Cottered Cranks

Though not en vogue on high-end bikes, there are

Fig. 11.8. Tightening or loosening a crank bolt attachment.

Fig. 11.9. Using Allan wrench to tighten, remove, or install a crank with one-key release.

Fig. 11.10. The crank bolt removed.

Fig. 11.11. Using crank tool to pull conventional cotterless crank off the axle.

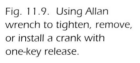

still some of these out there on older bikes, and they have to be maintained too. The bottom bracket used on these is usually of the same BSA type as the conventional one used with older cotterless cranks. So the only thing that's different is the attachment of the cranks to the bottom bracket axle.

If a cottered crank comes loose, it should be tightened immediately to prevent more damage. To tighten a cottered crank, support the crank close to the nut that's screwed on to the cotter pin on something solid, and firmly hit the cotter pin from the other side with a mallet or a hammer; then tighten the nut very firmly.

To remove a cottered crank (e.g., to gain access to the bearings), unscrew the nut and remove it and the underlying washer. Then, supporting the crank close to the cotter pin opposite the threaded side, place a thin block of hardwood on the end of the screw thread for protection, and hit it hard with a hammer until the cotter pin comes out the other side and you can push it through with e.g., a screwdriver. (More elegantly, it can be done with a special tool that works like a C-clamp to push the cotter pin out more gently.)

To reinstall a cottered crank, buy a new set of cotter pins of the right dimension. Clean and lightly grease all parts (hole in crank, grooved section of axle, and cotter pin). Install from the side of the crank with the larger diameter hole. Push the cotter pin in as far as possible, then hit it with a hammer, while supporting the crank close to the hole. Install the washer and the nut and tighten the nut fully. Tighten the nut again after an hour's riding, and two or three more times after that.

The Bottom Bracket

The bottom bracket is installed in the bottom bracket shell, i.e., the short piece of large-diameter tubing that runs perpendicular to the other tubes at the point where seat tube, down tube, and chain stays come together. It is the most heavily loaded set of ball bearings of the bike. The cranks are attached on either side.

These days, the bottom bracket is usually a self-contained unit, or cartridge, that gets installed in one piece. Older bottom brackets, and those on some cheaper bikes, may be of the type that has separate cup-and cone bearings, which (unlike the bearings of a cassette- type bottom bracket) can be adjusted, lubricated, and overhauled. The latter type comes in several different varieties: the BSA-type, found on most older road bikes and mountain bikes, the one that's often referred

Left: Fig. 11.12. Pulling a crank with a different tool.

Below: Fig. 11.14. Checking the bottom bracket bearings.

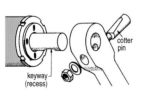

Fig. 11.13. Drawing of cottered crank connection.

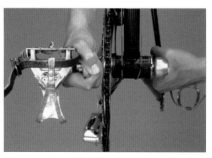

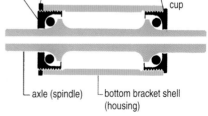

Fig. 11.15. Drawing of conventional bottom bracket.

to as Ashtabula that's found on cheap (American) cruisers and children's bikes, and the Thompson type used on some low-end German and East-European bikes.

Adjust, Lubricate, or Overhaul BSA Bottom Bracket

Do this work if the bearings feel either loose or tight. If they're loose, adjusting may be enough, but if they're tight, you should also lubricate the bearings. Adjusting can be done with the cranks still installed, while the left-hand crank must be removed to lubricate or

overhaul the bearings. See the preceding procedure for instructions on removing and reinstalling the cranks.

Tools and equipment:

- special bottom bracket tools

- ball bearing grease and cloth (if the bearing is to be lubricated or overhauled)

Adjusting procedure:

1. Using the matching tool, unscrew the notched lockring on the left-hand side of the bottom bracket by about one turn.

2. Using the pin wrench of the bottom bracket tools, tighten or loosen the left-hand bearing cup about $1/8$ of a turn.

3. Holding the bearing cup with the pin wrench, tighten the lockring firmly, making sure the bearing cup does not accidentally turn with it.

4. Check to make sure the adjustment is correct now and repeat, if necessary.

Disassembly procedure:

1. After at least the left-hand crank has been removed (preferably also the right-hand crank, and if not, then at least remove the chain off the chainring before you start), use the matching tool to remove the lockring on the left-hand side.

2. Using the pin wrench, remove the bearing cup on the left-hand side.

3. Remove the bearing balls (usually held in

Fig. 11.16. Removing or installing lockring on bottom bracket.

Fig. 11.17. Lockring removed from conventional bottom bracket, exposing the screw thread.

Fig. 11.18. Replacing the adjustable bearing cup.

Fig. 11.19. Replacing the bottom bracket axle.

a retainer) on the left-hand side.

4. Pull out the bottom bracket axle from the right-hand side, and catch the bearing balls (also usually in a retainer) on the right-hand side. Also remove the plastic sleeve that's usually installed inside the bottom bracket shell to keep dirt from the seat tube out of the bearings.

5. Unless you really want to replace the entire unit, stop here. Otherwise, also remove the bearing cup on the right-hand side, using the matching tool. Beware that this bearing usually has left-hand screw thread (except on some French bikes), so you have to turn it clockwise to remove it.

Overhauling procedure:

1. Clean and inspect all components and replace any damaged, pitted, or corroded items (it's a good idea to always replace the ball bearings, available as complete sets in retainers). The left-hand bearing cup can be inspected while on the bike — use a flashlight (torch in UK vernacular) to see the condition of the bearing surface — but it would have to be removed and replaced if it is damaged or badly worn (see Step 5 of the disassembly procedure above).

2. Fill the bearing cups with bearing grease and make sure the screw threads of bottom bracket shell, bearing cup(s), and lockring are clean; then apply some lubricant (preferably anti-seize lubricant) to the screw-threads.

3. Insert the bearing balls with the retainer in the grease-filled bearing cups, with the continuous side of the retainer facing into the bearing cup (facing out on the assembled bike).

4. Insert the bottom bracket axle from the left-hand side, followed by the plastic sleeve that is usually installed inside the shell to keep dirt out of the bearings.

5. Screw the left-hand bearing cup into the bottom bracket shell until the bearing is almost tight.

Fig. 11.20. Replacing the fixed bottom bracket bearing cup.

Fig. 11.22. Machine bearing, as used in most cartridge bearing bottom brackets.

Fig. 11.21. Lubricating the bearings in a conventional bottom bracket bearing cup.

Fig. 11.23. Manufacturer's photo of parts of a cartridge bearing assembly (Specialized).

6. Screw the lockring over the left-hand bearing cup and hold the latter with the pin wrench while tightening the lockring with the special wrench.

7. Check the bearing adjustment for smooth running before the cranks are installed, for play after the cranks are installed, and adjust if required.

Replace Cartridge Bearing Bottom Bracket

Do this work if a cartridge bearing bottom bracket is loose or does not turn smoothly. Both cranks must be removed first.

Tools and equipment:

- special bottom bracket tool(s) for the make and model in question

- special lockring wrench

Removal procedure:

1. Compare the two sides of the bottom bracket to check whether both sides have separate lockrings screwed over the top of a screw-threaded bearing adaptor, or only one side (while there's a one-piece adaptor on the other side. If there's only one lockring, note whether it's on the left- or the right-hand side, and make sure you assemble/disassemble working from the side with the lockring.

- Remove the lockring on the left-hand side if it's a unit with two lockrings or if it's a unit with the lockring on the left.

- If it's a single-lockring unit with the lockring on the right, remove that lockring.

- Unscrew the second lockring (if there is a lockring on the other side as well).

3. Unscrew the body of the bearing unit:

- if it's a single-lockring unit, always from the side opposite the lockring

- if it's a double-lockring unit, always from the right (chain side)

Note:

- If working from the right, you'll usually be dealing with left-hand thread (so you have to turn clockwise to remove, counterclockwise to install).

Installation procedure:

1. Make sure the new unit is designed for the same configuration as the old one and has the same axle length.

2. Clean and lightly lubricate (preferably with anti-seize lubricant) all screw threads, both in the bottom bracket shell and on the cartridge unit.

3. Screw the unit in from the side for which it is designed (usually from the left):

- if it's a single-lockring type, until the flange on the cartridge is hard up against the face of the bottom bracket shell

- if it's a double-lockring type, until the thread projects equally far on both sides

3. Install the lockring (or both lockrings if it's a double-lockring model) and tighten

Fig. 11.25. *Tightening the lockring against the bearing race.*

Fig. 11.24. Integral cartridge bearing bottom bracket.

well, holding the body of the unit with the matching pin wrench.

4. If it's a model with two lockrings, you may want to adjust the amount of projection on the two sides to be well balanced or to get as close as possible to the "ideal" chain line (as described in Chapter 13).

One-Piece Crankset

This type is found mainly on old-fashioned American cruisers and on low-end BMX and other children's bikes. As the name implies, the two crank arms are combined, together with the axle, as a single Z-shaped forged steel unit. They have to be adjusted about once a year, and whenever the bearings feel loose or tight.

Tools and equipment:

- screwdriver
- wrench to fit locknut

Procedure:

1. Loosen the locknut on the left-hand side turning clockwise (left-hand thread).

2. Lift the keyed washer that lies underneath and then use the screwdriver to adjust the cone — to the left to tighten, to the right to loosen the bearing.

3. Holding the cone in place with the screwdriver, tighten the locknut counterclockwise.

Notes:

- If the unit needs to be lubricated, you can gain access to the bearings by unscrewing the locknut and the cone all the way.

At this point, you can push the Z-shaped unit out to the chain side of the bottom bracket shell, exposing the right-hand bearing. Clean all parts before lubricating with grease. Then assemble again. To do this job more thoroughly, you'd have to remove the left-hand pedal, which allows you to push the whole unit out to the chain side, giving you a chance to thoroughly clean, inspect, lubricate, and/ or replace individual components.

- On these one-piece cranks, the chainring is held onto a threaded portion of the crank arm unit with a nut and an engagement peg on the inside of the right-hand crank arm. Undo the nut to remove the chainring.

Thompson-Type Bottom Bracket

This type, mainly found on older low-end European bikes, is shown in Fig. 11.27. To adjust the bearing, first loosen the locknut on the left-hand side by turning clockwise (left-hand thread). Then simply turn the underlying dust cap, which engages the cone underneath — to the right to loosen, to the left to tighten the bearing.

If you need to gain access to the bearing, the cranks must be removed first. Then unscrew and remove the locknut, the washer, and the cone, after which the entire unit will come out on the chain side. Do the usual cleaning, inspection, and lubrication, and reassemble in reverse order, keeping in mind that the screw thread is left-handed.

Left: Fig. 11.26. Adjusting a one-piece crank bottom bracket bearing

Right: Fig. 11.27. Adjusting details of Thompson bottom bracket bearing.

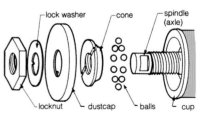

The Chainrings

On derailleur bicycles, two or three chainrings are installed on the right-hand crank. They usually come in a standard combination with respect to the numbers of teeth. They must be designed for the particular make and model of the crankset, because the number of attachment bolts, as well as the distance relative to each other, can differ quite a bit.

Under normal circumstances, the chainrings do not wear very much and will hold up quite long. However, they may have to be replaced if they see a lot of hard use, especially in bad weather and muddy terrain, or if they get damaged. On non-derailleur bikes, there's only one chainring, and it's often permanently at-

tached to the right-hand crank (in which case it can only be replaced together with the crank, following the instructions above for crank replacement).

Tighten Chainrings

In conjunction with the annual inspection (and preferably even the monthly inspection), the chainrings may have to be tightened if one or more of the installation bolts is loose. It's also one of the possible causes for unpredictable shifting of derailleur gears.

Tools and equipment:

• Allan wrench and a slotted wrench specifically designed to fit the attachment bolts

Procedure:

1. Holding each of the bolts in the back of the chainring in turn with the slotted wrench, tighten the corresponding Allan bolt from the front, gradually working around until all bolts (usually four or five) have been tightened.

   • Replace any bolts that cannot be tightened with new ones (both parts of the bolt).

   • On triple-chainring units, there is usually a second set of bolts, accessible only from the back, holding the smallest chainring — check and tighten those bolts as well.

Replace Chainrings

Do this if a chainring is damaged or worn: however, sometimes you'll merely want to remove the chainrings so you can give them a more thorough cleaning, without need to actually replace them with new ones. Do this work either with the right-hand crank still installed on the bike or with the crank removed. Remove the chain from the chainring before starting this work.

Tools and equipment:

• Allan wrench and a slotted wrench specifically designed to fit the attachment bolts

Removal procedure:

1. Holding each of the bolts in the back of the chainring in turn with the slotted

Left:
Fig. 11.28. Chainrings mounted on the right-hand crank of high-end mountain bike.

Right:
Fig. 11.29. Removing or installing chainrings.

Below: Fig. 11.30. Replacing the bolts that hold the chainrings.

Left:
Fig. 11.31.
Straighten-
ing chain-
ring teeth.

Right:
Fig. 11.32.
This way,
you can
sometimes
straighten
a bent
chainring.

wrench, loosen the corresponding Allan bolt from the front, removing both parts, gradually working around until all bolts (usually either four or five) have been removed.

- On triple-chainring units, there is usually a second set of bolts, accessible only from the back, holding the smallest chainring — remove those bolts as well. If not, the whole set of three chainrings stays together as a unit.

2. Remove the chainrings, either separately (in which case there will also be spacers to catch) or as a unit.

Installation procedure:

1. Compare with the original configuration how the unit is assembled (you may have to do that before installing them to the crank's chainring attachment arms).

2. Attach one bolt (with spacer) and the other part of the bolt holding the chainring(s) to the attachment, but do not tighten it fully yet.

3. Do the same with another bolt roughly opposite the first one.

4. Install the other bolts.

5. Gradually tighten all bolts fully.

Notes:

- Replace any bolts that cannot be tightened

fully, making sure they're the right length

- On modern bikes with special tooth patterns, the chainrings have to stay lined up the same way (because they're shaped that way to aid shifting). Check for an alignment mark to install them correctly

Straighten Chainring and Chainring Teeth

If either the chainring or one or more of the teeth are bent, you may be able to correct the situation by bending it back. But replace the whole chainring (or the whole riveted-together set of chainrings, if that's the way they come on your bike) if a tooth breaks or is permanently deformed — or when the chainring itself is so seriously bent that the tool won't straighten it. Before you start, remove the chain

from the chainring (see Chapter 13 for instructions).

Tools and equipment:

- special chainring or chainring tooth tool (or in a pinch, an adjustable wrench)

Procedure:

1. Fit the tool exactly over the tooth or the bent section of chainring as far as it will go without also grabbing beyond the location of the bend, and then use it to straighten the tooth or the chainring.

2. Check the result and repeat, if necessary (but replace the entire chainring(s) if a tooth remains seriously bent, cracks, or breaks — or if the chainring just can't be straightened).

CHAPTER 12

Pedal Maintenance

Pedals come in two basic types — conventional and clipless. Conventional pedals can be used with regular footwear, while clipless pedals require special shoes equipped with matching clips. (Yes, "clipless" is a bit of a misnomer for the type of pedal that *does* require a special clip on the shoe sole.)

They also come with one of two bearing types: cartridge or cup-and-cone bearings. You can tell them apart as follows: If there's a removable dust cap on the outside end of the pedal, it's probably a conventional (adjustable) type; if not, it's definitely a cartridge-bearing type. (Actually, there's a third bearing type too: sleeve bearings, as found on really cheap bikes; the only advice on those is to replace them with better pedals running on ball bearings if they give you trouble.) Clipless pedals always have cartridge bearings, while conventional pedals may be of either type.

The pedals are screwed into the threaded holes at the end of the cranks. The left-hand pedal has left-hand screw thread (and is usually marked with an "L"), while the right-hand pedal has regular right-hand screw thread. If you're having difficulty tightening or loosening a pedal, first check whether you're turning them the right way or not — left-hand thread means tighten counterclockwise and loosen clockwise. And remember that the right-hand crank is the one on the chain side.

Pedal adjustment or overhauling will be called for if the pedal either feels loose or does not turn freely. If it wobbles, there's a more serious problem — the axle is bent. In that case, re-place either the pedal axle (if available) or the whole pedal.

The release force of clipless pedals can be adjusted to suit your needs. If you use conventional pedals, you may want to use them in conjunction with "old-fashioned" toe-clips. Check and tighten their attachment screws to the front of the pedal occasionally to stop them from coming loose.

The other items you'll often find on a conventional pedal are little reflectors. Also check and tighten their

Top right: Fig. 12.2. Conventional pedal.

Bottom right: Fig. 12.3. Clipless pedal.

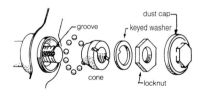

Fig. 12.1. Bearing details of conventional pedal.

attachments from time to time, and replace them if missing or broken.

With all pedal work, you should work on only one at a time. That's because some identical-looking parts of the two pedals are actually not identical and you would do serious damage if you mixed them up.

Replace Pedals

This work can be called for if the pedal is damaged — or when the bike has to be stored in a small box, e.g., to be transported. Note that the pedal wrench used for this work may either be the metric size 15 mm or the non-metric size $9/16$ inch.

Tools and equipment:

- pedal wrench (or, if not too tight, a (preferably long) 6 mm Allan wrench)

up to left   up to right

left-hand thread   right-hand thread

Fig. 12.4.
Pedal screw thread detail.

- lubricant
- cloth

Removal procedure:

1. Place the pedal wrench on the flat surfaces of the stub between the pedal and the crank. (If the pedal is not on too tight, it can usually be done with the Allan wrench, reaching the hexagonal recess that's present in the end of most modern pedals from the back of the crank.)

2. Hold the crank arm firmly and:

   - for the right-hand pedal, turn coun-

Fig. 12.5.
Removing or installing pedal with pedal wrench.

terclockwise to loosen

   - for the left-hand pedal, turn clockwise

3. Unscrew the pedal all the way.

Installation procedure:

1 Clean the thread surfaces in the cranks and on the pedals, and lubricate them lightly.

2. Carefully align the thread of the pedal stub with the thread in the crank and start screwing it in by hand (counterclockwise for the left-hand pedal).

3. Screw in the pedal fully with the pedal wrench (or from the back of the crank,

Fig. 12.6.
Using Allan wrench to install or remove pedal.

using the Allan wrench). There's no need to tighten them excessively.

Adjust Release Force of Clipless Pedal

If it is too hard to get your foot out of a clipless pedal, or if it does not hold the shoe firmly enough, you can adjust the spring tension.

Tools and equipment:

- Allan wrench to fit the adjustment bolt(s)

Procedure

1. Locate the tension adjustment bolt or bolts on the pedal in question.

Fig. 12.7.
Applying lubricant to pedal screw thread before installing pedal in crank.

2. Tighten or loosen the bolt(s) as required.

3. Check operation and fine-tune adjustment, if necessary.

Adjust Conventional Pedal Bearings

This work can usually be done with the pedal still attached to the bike. However, if the pedal has a cage that wraps around, it may be necessary to remove the cage to gain access to the outboard bearing.

Tools and equipment:

- tool to remove dust cap
- open-ended wrench and/or socket wrench
- small screwdriver

Procedure:

1. Holding the pedal at the crank, loosen the dust cap (it's usually threaded but may be snapped on, in which case you'll have to pry it off).

2. Unscrew the locknut by about one turn.

3. Using whatever tool fits the cone (the small screwdriver if

the top of the cone is slotted), turn the cone in or out by about ¼ turn to tighten or loosen the bearing, respectively.

4. Holding the cone with the screwdriver, tighten the locknut.

5. Check the adjustment of the bearing and fine-tune the adjustment, if necessary, making sure the locknut is firmed up properly.

6. Reinstall the dust cap.

Lubricate and Overhaul Conventional Pedal

Although this work can be done with the pedal still on the bike, it's recommended to remove it first — and reinstall it afterwards. If the pedal has a cage that wraps

Left: Fig. 12.8. Adjusting clipless pedal release force.

around, it may be necessary to remove the cage to gain access to the outboard bearing.

Because some pedal parts are not interchangeable between left and right, you should keep all the parts separate or work on only one pedal at a time.

Tools and equipment:

- tool to remove dust cap
- open-ended wrench and/or socket wrench
- small screwdriver
- cloth
- bearing grease

Disassembly procedure:

1. Holding the pedal at the crank, loosen the dust cap (it's usually threaded, but may be

Below: Fig. 12.11. Well-greased cup-and-cone pedal bearing.

Left: Fig. 12.9. Locknut on conventional cup-and-cone pedal bearing.

Left: Fig. 12.10. This pedal cone can be adjusted with a screwdriver.

snapped on, in which case you'll be able to pry it off).

2. Unscrew the locknut and remove it; then also remove the keyed washer.

3. Using whatever tool fits the cone (the small screwdriver if the top of the cone is slotted), unscrew and remove the cone.

Above: Fig. 12.12. Conventional pedal with cup-and-cone bearings taken apart.

Below: Fig. 12.13. Removing the cage on a conventional pedal.

4. Pull the pedal body and the pedal axle apart, catching all the bearing balls.

Overhauling and reassembly procedure:

1. Clean and inspect all parts, replacing any that are pitted, corroded, or otherwise damaged. It's always a good idea to replace the bearing balls, which on pedals are not held in a retainer.

2. Fill both bearing cups with bearing grease, and push the bearing balls in.

3. Slide the pedal body back over the axle, with the larger bearing cup toward the crank; be careful not to push the ball bearings out.

4. Install the cone until the bearing feels just barely loose.

5. Install the keyed washer with the tab matching the groove (replace it if it is worn so much that it can slip out of the groove).

6. Install the locknut and tighten it against the cone.

7. Check the bearing adjustment and fine-tune it, if necessary.

8. Install the dust cap.

Maintenance of Cartridge-Bearing Pedal

You can do this work either with the pedal still installed on the bike or removed. Because some pedal parts are not interchangeable between left and right, you should keep all the parts separate or work on only one pedal at a time.

Fig. 12.14. Unscrewing the cartridge from a clipless cartridge-bearing pedal.

Tools and equipment:

- wrench to fit the flat hexagonal stub that screws into the pedal body

- cloth

- lubricant

Disassembly procedure

1. Holding the hexagon stub that's screwed into the back of the pedal body with the wrench, unscrew the pedal body off by hand. (It may have either right- or left-hand screw thread.)

2. Pull off the pedal body. You have now separated the pedal axle with one (inner) bearing from the pedal body with the other (outer) bearing.

Fig. 12.15. Parts of a typical clipless cartridge bearing pedal.

3. Check to see whether there is access to the pedal body that allows you to remove the outer bearing — and do so if you can (otherwise, a special tool will be needed, and you should leave this job to a bike mechanic).

Overhauling and assembly procedure:

1. Check the condition of any parts you can see. If the axle is bent, replace the entire cartridge (if available — if not, you'll have to replace the pedals).

2. If you can remove the bearings, do so. If not, try to lift the bearing seals to gain access to them.

3. Lubricate the bearings and reinstall the parts on the spindle, or axle.

4. Reinstall any parts you removed and reinsert the cartridge into the pedal body.

5. Screw the cartridge in all the way.

Toe-Clip Installation

Except for rubber-block type pedals found on city cruisers, most conventional pedals lend themselves to the installation of toe-clips, which makes riding more comfortable, especially on longer trips.

Tools and equipment:

- screwdriver

- 7 mm open-ended wrench

Installation procedure:

1. Establish which end is the front of the pedal, and remove the reflector, if installed there.

2. Place the toe-clip on the front of the pedal, with the closed end facing forward and up, then install the screws and the nuts (and washers, if provided).

   - If the reflector lends itself to installation over the top of the toe-clip, put it back on.

3. Insert the toe strap from the outside of the pedal, through the slots in the pedal

Fig. 12.16. Installation of toe-clip on a conventional pedal.

(twisting it between the two pedal sides if possible to restrain it), then up and through the opening in the toe-clip, and hook the end into the buckle.

CHAPTER 13

Chain Maintenance

The bicycle chain consists of an array of chain links, connected by means of pins. Each neighboring set of link pins is connected with side plates and bushings around the pins reduce the friction.

Chain Sizes and Types

Two sizes are used for bicycles, referring to the length and inside width of a link, measured between subsequent links and inside the inner side plates, respectively. Derailleur bicycles take chains of the nominal dimension $\frac{1}{2}$ x $\frac{3}{32}$ inch,

while non-derailleur bikes, especially those with coaster brakes, usually take the slightly wider chains of nominal dimension $\frac{1}{2}$ x $\frac{1}{8}$ inch.

Actually, the dimension of the derailleur chain is no longer as standardized as it once was. With the advent of 8-, 9-, and now even 10-speed freewheels, there is less space between them to accommodate a normal chain, so chains for these are

narrower and may be identified by their inside width in mm.

When replacing a chain, or when adding links to an existing chain, it will be very important to get one that is identical, and that may involve not only the width, but also the design of the chain. The big word to keep in mind is "Hyperglide" — that's the standard for Shimano's narrow specially-shaped freewheel cogs, and the chain for bikes thus equipped must be "Hyperglide compatible." It does not have to be a Shimano chain, because Hyperglide-compatible Sedis (now SRAM) chains work just as well.

The way the ends of the chain are connected differs for the two types: the wider chain for non-derailleur bikes is joined by means of a so-called

master link, as shown in Figs. 13.3 and 13.16, while the narrower derailleur chain is joined the same way as in which all the pins connect subsequent links. To connect or disconnect the derailleur chain, one of the pins is pushed out far enough to free the inside link plate and back in again. To shorten a chain, a pin is pushed out all the way, so the last one or more links on the other side of that pin just drop out.

Chain Line

That's the path the chain takes relative to the centerline through the length of the bike. It's most efficient, and least

Fig. 13.1. The chain mating with a chainring.

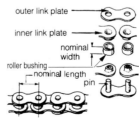

Fig. 13.2. Chain detail drawing.

outer link plate

inner link plate

nominal width

roller bushing

nominal length

pin

Fig. 13.3. Derailleur chain with special connecting link (the brassy one).

troublesome, when the chain runs exactly parallel. In reality, it will vary quite a bit from this "ideal" chain line when you shift gears on a derailleur bike, making it marginally less efficient. To keep these variations to an acceptable minimum (and more importantly, to aid gear shifting), the chain should preferably be run so that it follows the ideal chain line when the center between the two or three chainrings is lined up with the center between the biggest and smallest cog in the back.

General Chain Maintenance

As far as chain maintenance is concerned, the main things to consider are cleaning, lubrication, and the amount of wear (which leads to apparent "stretch"). If you ride off-road a lot, the chain should probably be replaced every six months or so; otherwise, once a year should be enough.

To check for wear, recommended at least once a year, use either a special chain wear tool or measure a 50-link stretch of chain to see whether it has apparently "stretched" to the point where it's 25½ inches, rather than the 25 inches

a new 50-link section should measure.

The best way to clean a chain is to remove it and rinse it out in a mixture of solvent with 5–10% mineral oil, brushing and rinsing it thoroughly. Then hang it out to dry (the mineral oil that was dissolved stays behind, inhibiting rust when the solvent evaporates). In dry climates, the best lubricants are wax-based, whereas in wet weather you're better off with a grease-based lubricant for the chain. The easiest way to apply the lubricant is with a spray can or a special dispenser with a brush at the end.

As a result of an accident or maltreatment of the bike (e.g., when transporting or storing it), one or more links of a chain may be bent or twisted. This will seriously affect shifting on a derailleur bike — replace the links in question or the entire chain.

Chain Replacement

This work is required if the old chain is worn and in order to clean the existing chain. The description is based on a derailleur bike, while notes at the end of the description explain what to consider on a bike without derailleurs. As for which chain to choose, that depends on the cogs on the back: consult with a bike shop to make sure you get a

Fig. 13.7. Bent chain link — must be replaced.

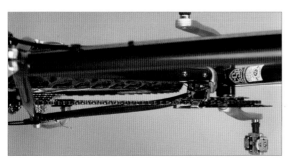

Top left: Fig. 13.4. Connecting link for use on non-derailleur bikes.

Top right: Fig. 13.5. Normally, derailleur chains are separated by pushing out one of the pins.

Bottom left: Fig. 13.6. Chain line.

chain suitable for the combination of cogs on your bike.

Tools and equipment:

- chain rivet tool
- cloths

Removal procedure:

1. While turning the cranks by the pedals, with the rear wheel lifted off the ground, select the gear in which the chain runs over the smallest cog in the rear and the smallest chainring in the front.

2. Turn back the handle of the chain rivet tool (counterclockwise), so the pin of the tool is retracted all the way. Then place the tool between two links, with the pin of the tool firmly up against the chain link pin.

3. Turn the handle in (clockwise) firmly, pushing the chain link pin out; but don't push the pin out all the way (it will be practically impossible to replace the pin if you push it out all the way) — just far enough so no more than $1/32$ inch (about 0.5 mm) of the pin stays engaged.

4. Turn the handle back (counterclockwise) until it comes free of the chain, and remove the tool.

5. Wiggle the chain links apart at the point of the retracted chain link pin.

Installation procedure:

1. Select the gear by which the chain engages the smallest cog in the back and the smallest chainring in the front.

2. Working from the chain end that does not have the pin sticking out, wrap the chain around the chainring, through the front derailleur cage, around the small rear cog, and over and between the derailleur pulleys as shown in Fig. 13.13, until the two ends of the chain can be connected.

3. Place the slight inward protrusion of the pin that was pushed out over the inner link that forms the other end of the chain, and hold the two parts in place correctly aligned.

4. Turn the handle of the chain tool back far enough for the pin on the tool to clear the protruding end of the pin on the chain, and then turn it in until there is firm contact between the two pins.

5. While continuing to hold the two chain links properly aligned, turn the handle of the chain tool in, pushing the chain link pin in all the way until it protrudes equally far on both sides; then remove the tool.

6. Apply sideways force, twisting in both directions, until the two chain links around the newly replaced pin rotate freely. If it

Fig. 13.8. Using chain tool to push out link pin.

Fig. 13.9. The pin being pushed out.

Fig. 13.10. Twisting the chain at the joint to free the pushed-out link pin.

can't be done this way, put the chain tool on from the opposite side and push the chain link pin back in slightly.

- On relatively wide chains (i.e., those not intended for use with 8-, 9-, and 10-speed cassettes), the connection can usually be loosened by using the chain tool in its second position, which pushes the links apart.

Note:

- If the pin is accidentally pushed all the way out during disassembly, you can remove the last two links and replace them with a new two-link section of chain — taking care not to lose the pin again.

Hyperglide note:

- On Shimano's Hyperglide chains, there is one slightly bigger link with a black finish (compared to the shiny bright appearance of the rest of

the chain). That's the only pin to disconnect and connect the chain (of course, to shorten the chain, you'll break it at a different link, but you'll still connect at the black pin). That pin has to be discarded when removed and replaced by a new one, which has an extension that has to be cut off after installation.

- Use Shimano's special tool for working on Hyperglide chains, and keep a couple of spare black pins around.

Chain Length

On a derailleur bike, the chain should be just long enough to wrap around the biggest chainring and the biggest cog, while still leaving enough spring tension at the derailleur — and short enough not to hang loose while it runs over the smallest cog and the smallest chainring. (If that can't be achieved, you need a rear derailleur on which the pulleys are farther apart, known as a wide-range or long-cage derailleur.

On a non-derailleur bike, the chain length

Top left: Fig. 13.11. The chain taken apart at the pushed-out pin.

Top right: Fig. 13.14. Twisting the chain to free a stiff connection.

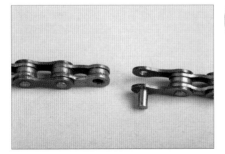

Fig. 13.13. Chain routing at the rear derailleur.

Bottom left: Fig. 13.15. Using the chain tool to push the pin back in.

Bottom right: Fig. 13.15. Using the special chain tool on a Hyperglide chain.

97

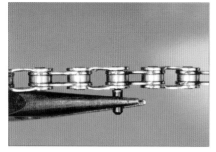

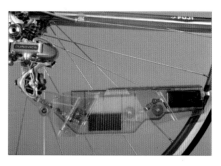

Left:
Fig. 13.15. Breaking off the exposed end of a special Hyperglide connecting pin.

Right:
Fig. 13.17. Special tool for cleaning and lubricating a chain while on the bike.

Chain rotation direction

Fig. 13.16. Master link for non-derailleur chain.

should be such that there is about ¾ inch (2 cm) up-and-down movement possible in the middle of the free chain between cog and chainring. You can make minor adjustments by moving the rear wheel back or forth a little and clamping it in properly. On a wheel with hub brake, this also requires you to loosen the counter lever and retighten it in the right position once the wheel bolts are tightened.

Major corrections of the chain length (for derailleur and non-derailleur bikes alike) are made by removing or adding a section of chain consisting of an even number of links. Follow essentially the same procedure described above for chain removal and installation.

Chains With Master Link

The wider chain used on many non-derailleur bicycles can be opened up and connected by means of the special so-called master link provided with these chains. It is built up as shown in Fig. 13.16. Remove it by prying off the spring clip with e.g., a small screwdriver (covering it with a cloth, so you don't lose the small spring). Then the loose link plate can be lifted off and the rest of the link (the fixed link plate with the two pins attached) comes out from the other side of the chain. When installing a master link, make sure the direction of rotation of the chain is such that the closed end of the spring clip points forward in the direction of chain rotation.

Finally, if the chain is too loose or too tight (more or less than about ¾ inch, or 2 cm, up-and- down movement in the middle between chainring and cog), loosen the rear wheel and slide it back or forward, then retighten it. On a wheel with hub brake, this would also require you to loosen the counter lever and retighten it in the right position once the wheel is installed.

CHAPTER 14

Derailleur Gearing Maintenance

Most adult bikes sold these days are equipped with derailleur gearing, and this chapter addresses maintenance of these systems. The derailleur system consists of a rear derailleur and a front derailleur, controlled by means of shifters to which the derailleurs are connected by means of gear control cables.

The rear derailleur selects one of 7 to 10 cogs on the rear freewheel with different numbers of teeth, and the front derailleur selects one of 2 or 3 different size chainrings in the front.

The shifters may be either on the handlebars or on the frame's down tube. Modern road bikes are typically shifted by means of ratcheted levers integrated with the brake levers, although separate shifters for down tube installation are still available. Mountain bikes and other machines with flat handlebars are either shifted by means of a rotating twist grip or by means of shift levers mounted under the handlebars, just inboard from the brake levers.

Think of derailleur gearing as a system, because if there is a problem, it may be due to any of a number of factors ranging from the derailleur mechanism to the cable to the shifter — in fact, even the chain or the cogs and chainrings may be at fault. Keep that in mind when troubleshooting for gearing problems. None of the components require much in the way of maintenance other than keeping them clean and occasionally adjusting.

The chainrings were described in Chapter 11; the other components of the gearing system will be covered here.

As for terminology, this text adheres to the manufacturers' preferred nomenclature. In the UK, the front derailleur is often called a "changer," while the rear derailleur is often referred to as a "mech," short for mechanism.

The Rear Derailleur

Take a look at the rear derailleur. It consists of a metal cage with two little wheels, or pulleys, over which the chain is guided, and a spring-tensioned parallelogram

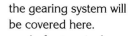

Fig. 14.3. Rear derailleur in the process of moving the chain from one cog to another.

Fig. 14.2. Manufacturer's rendition of a rear derailleur (Shimano).

Left: Fig. 14.1. Derailleur gearing system on a modern 27-speed bike.

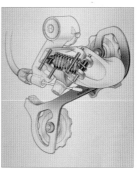

mechanism that moves the cage sideways to line up with the different cogs on the freewheel at the rear wheel hub. Note the various adjusting screws sticking out at different points and the adjusting barrel for the cable tension.

The two most common problems at the rear derailleur are over- or undershifting and failure to index properly at the gear selected. Both these problems can usually be overcome with simple adjustments. Overshifting occurs when the chain is shifted too far in the highest or the lowest gear, getting caught between the smallest cog and the frame or between the biggest cog and the wheel, respectively. Undershifting occurs

when the chain doesn't get shifted far enough at the smallest or the biggest cog, so the corresponding gear cannot be engaged.

Failure to index properly occurs when the chain doesn't line up with the cog, so the gear does not engage correctly — either skipping gears or running in gear with a scraping noise. The most common problem, improper indexing, is adjusted easily with the cable adjusting barrel on the derailleur.

Adjust Rear Derailleur

When the gears do not engage properly, it's a good idea to first make sure the cable is in good condition (and replace it

if it isn't). Then proceed as follows to adjust:

Tools and equipment:

• Usually none required (sometimes a wrench to fit the cable clamp bolt)

Procedure:

1. Place the bike in an intermediate gear.

2. Locate the adjusting mechanism at the point where the control cable enters the derailleur.

3. Turn the adjuster out in ½-turn increments and try shifting through the entire range of gears, while turning the cranks with the wheel lifted off the ground. Note whether the problem gets better or worse.

   • If the problem got better, continue adjusting in small increments until the derailleur indexes properly.

   • If the problem got worse, turn the adjuster in the opposite direction until the derailleur indexes properly.

4. If you can't turn the adjuster in or out far enough:

   • Use the additional adjuster at the shifter that may be present on bikes with flat handle-bars.

   • Select the highest gear, i.e., the smallest cog, then clamp the cable in at a different point with the wrench, using the needle-nose pliers to pull the cable taut.

5. If the highest or lowest gear cannot be reached properly, or the chain shifts beyond the gear, refer to *Over- and Under-shift Adjustment* below.

Fig. 14.4. Rear derailleur in low-gear position.

Fig. 14.5. Rear derailleur in high-gear position.

Fig. 14.6. Adjusting the gears at the rear derailleur.

Angle Adjustment Note:

• On most modern derailleurs, there is a separate adjustment screw near the derailleur mounting point, to adjust the limiting angle of the derailleur cage relative to the horizontal plane. You may try adjusting this one way or the other, bringing the chain and the upper pulley (called "jockey pulley") closer to, or farther from, the cogs.

Over- and Undershift Adjustment

This problem is particularly prevalent after the rear wheel or the cogs on the rear wheel have

Fig. 14.7. Adjusting derailleur at an intermediate point on a road bike with integrated brake-shifting devices.

been replaced. However, it can also be due to either normal wear or damage in an accident (in which case you should first check for, and correct, any damage).

Tools and equipment:

• small screwdriver

Procedure:

1. Find the two small adjusting screws that limit the sideways travel of the derailleur cage. Usually, one is marked "H" for high, limiting travel toward the high gear (outside, smallest cog), the other one "L" for low, limiting travel toward the low gear (inside, biggest cog).

   • If they're not marked, place the bike in the highest or the lowest gear (smallest or biggest cog in the

rear) and establish which is which by turning one of them in (clockwise) to find out whether that results in less movement to the outside (so that would be "H") or the inside (so that would be "L").

2. Depending on the problem, turn the relevant adjusting screw in or out in ½-turn increments:

   • Turn the "H" screw in to compensate for overshifting at the high gear (i.e., the chain was shifted beyond the smallest cog), or out to compensate for undershifting at the high end (i.e., the chain did not quite reach that smallest cog).

   • Turn the "L" screw in to compensate for overshifting at

the low gear (i.e., the chain was shifted beyond the largest cog), or out to compensate for undershifting at the low end (i.e., the chain did not quite reach that largest cog).

3. Lift the wheel off the ground and turn the crank, shifting into all the gears, and fine-tune the adjustment until it works the way it should.

Note:

Also see the *Angle Adjustment Note* above.

Rear Derailleur Maintenance

Before starting with this work, you may want to undo the cable attach-

Fig. 14.9. Adjusting derailleur at a twist-grip type shifter.

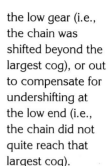

Left:
Fig. 14.8. Adjusting derailleur at the shifter on a mountain bike.

ment at the derailleur — however, then you'll have to readjust the system afterwards. Usually, the work can be done with the derailleur still attached to its cable.

Tools and equipment:

- Allan wrenches (or regular wrenches for older models)
- cloths
- solvent and lubricant

Procedure:

1. Remove the bolt that holds the lower pulley.

2. Remove the lower pulley (the tension wheel); now the chain can be removed from the derailleur cage.

3. Also remove the other pulley (the jockey wheel).

4. Clean, inspect, and lubricate all parts. Replace the pulleys if they can't be made to turn freely.

5. Reinstall the jockey wheel.

6. Put the chain back in the cage.

7. Install the tension wheel.

8. Check operation and make any adjustments necessary per the preceding procedures.

Replace Rear Derailleur

The rear derailleur on modern quality bikes is held by means of an Allan mounting bolt, which attaches it to an extension of the right-hand dropout called "derailleur eye." On cheap bikes, it may be attached to a separate mounting plate held between the hub and the dropout. Make sure the new derailleur is designed for the particular range of cogs on your wheel. To handle big gearing steps, you need a wide-range derailleur, characterized by a big cage — with the pulleys far apart

Tools and equipment

- Allan wrenches, sometimes (for older derailleurs), just one Allan wrench and a 7 mm open-ended or box wrench.

Removal procedure:

1. Put the rear derailleur in the highest gear (smallest cog) and remove the cable, following the procedure for cable replacement.

2. Remove the jockey pulley to free the chain (alternately, you can disconnect the chain, following the procedure in Chapter 13).

3. Remove the mounting bolt, and take the derailleur off the bike.

Installation procedure:

1. Install the mounting bolt, while pushing the derailleur up against the spring

Fig. 14.12. Lubricating the derailleur pulleys.

Fig. 14.10. Adjusting the range limit screws at the rear derailleur.

Fig. 14.11. Adjusting the angle limit stop screw at the rear derailleur.

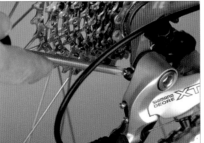

tension so that it clears the derailleur eye (or the mounting plate).

2. If necessary, remove the tension wheel, then slide the chain in, and reinstall the tension wheel.

3. Attach the cable.

Above: Fig. 14.13. Lubricating the derailleur mechanism.

Below: Fig. 14.14. Removing or installing the tension wheel pivot bolt.

4. Make any adjustments that may be necessary, following the procedures above.

Adjust Front Derailleur

When the gears do not engage properly in the front, first make sure the cable is in good condition (and replace it if it isn't). Then proceed as follows to adjust:

Tools and equipment:

• Usually none required (sometimes a wrench to fit the cable clamp bolt)

Procedure:

1. Select the gear that combines the middle

Fig. 14.15. Removing or installing the tension wheel.

chainring with an intermediate cog.

2. Locate the adjusting mechanism at the point where the control cable enters the derailleur.

3. Turn the adjuster out in ½-turn increments, and try shifting through the entire range of gears, turning the cranks with the wheel lifted off the ground. Note whether the problem gets better or worse.

• If the problem got better, continue adjusting in ½-turn increments until the derailleur indexes properly.

• If the problem got worse, turn the adjuster in the opposite direction until the derailleur indexes properly.

3. If there is not enough adjustment to solve the problem:

• Use the additional adjuster at the shifter that may be present on bikes with flat handlebars.

• If still no luck, elect the highest gear, i.e., the largest chainring, then clamp the cable in at a different point with the wrench, using the needle-nose pliers to pull the cable taut.

5. If the highest or lowest gear cannot be reached properly, or the chain shifts beyond the gear, refer to *Over- and Undershift Adjustment* below.

Right: Fig. 14.16. Removing or installing the derailleur mounting bolt.

Over- and Undershift Adjustment

When this problem occurs at the front derailleur, it may either be due to normal wear or damage in an accident (in which case you should first check for, and correct, any damage).

Tools and equipment:

- small screwdriver

Fig. 14.17. Clamping in the control cable.

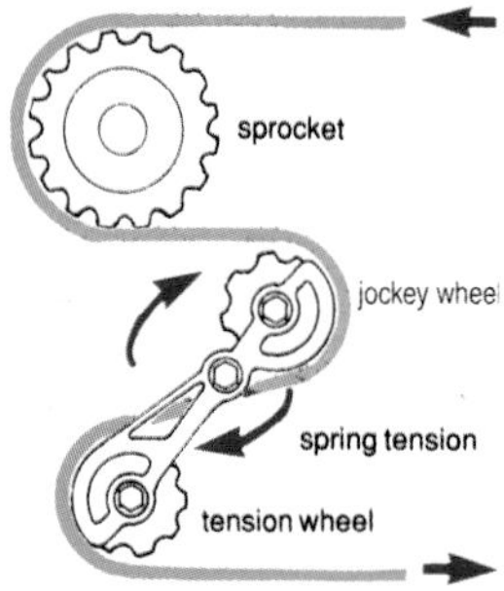

Procedure:

1. Find the two small adjusting screws that limit the sideways travel of the derailleur cage. Usually, one is marked "H" for high, limiting travel toward the high gear (outside, large chainring), the other one "L" for low, limiting travel toward the low gear (inside, small chainring).

   - If they're not marked, establish which is which by

Fig. 14.19. Drawing of chain routing at rear derailleur.

turning one of them in (clockwise) to find out whether that results in less movement to the inside (so that would be "L") or the outside (so that would be "H").

2. Depending on the problem, turn the relevant adjusting screw in or out in ½-turn increments:

   - Turn the "H" screw in to compensate for overshifting at the high gear (i.e., the chain was shifted beyond the largest chainring), or out to compensate for undershifting at the high end (i.e., the chain did not quite reach

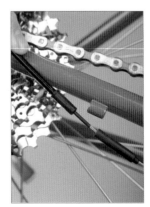

Fig. 14.20. Cable routing at cable stop on frame.

that largest chainring).

   - Turn the "L" screw in to compensate for overshifting at the low gear (i.e., the chain was shifted beyond the smallest chainring), or out to compensate for undershifting at the low end (i.e., the chain did not quite reach that smallest chainring).

3. Lift the wheel off the ground and turn the crank, shifting into all the gears, and fine-tune the adjustment until it works the way it should.

Fig. 14.21. Adjusting the range limit stop screw at the front derailleur.

Left:
Fig. 14.18. Derailleur removed, showing derailleur eye on the frame.

Replace Derailleur Cable

Replace the cable if it is hard to move, either because it is corroded or damaged, e.g., is pinched, kinked, or frayed. Whether for the front or the rear derailleur, the procedure is the same. If it's an indexed derailleur, buy a cable for the particular derailleur on your bike (yes, nowadays they're quite specific); if not, just make sure it's a cable with the right type of nipple (check at the shifter what shape and size it has). Before you start, put the bike in the gear that engages the smallest cog in the rear or the smallest chainring in the front.

Tools and equipment:

- wrench for cable clamp at derailleur
- needle-nose pliers
- cable cutters
- sometimes diagonal cutters
- cloth and lubricant (preferably wax)

Procedure:

1. Undo the cable clamp bolt at the derailleur.

2. At the shifter, pull the outer cable back a little and then push the inner cable in toward the shifter to expose the nipple at the shifter and enough

cable to reach that point with the pliers.

3. Pull the cable out, first with the pliers, then by hand, catching the various sections of outer cable at the shifter and (on a rear derailleur) at the derailleur.

4. Make sure the new cable and the outer cable sections are of the same type and length as the original. Then apply some lubricant to the inner cable.

5. Starting at the shifter, install the inner cable through the shifter, the outer cable sec-

tions, over or through any guides on the frame, and into the derailleur itself.

6. Clamp the cable end provisionally (i.e., not too tight yet).

7. Try the gears, turning the cranks with the wheel lifted off the ground, and adjust the cable (both with the adjuster and with the cable clamp bolt) until all gears work properly — refer to the preceding procedures *Adjust Rear Derailleur* and *Adjust Front Derailleur*.

Fig. 14.23. Cable and nipple (loosened) at a conventional down-tube shifter.

Fig. 14.22. Clamping in the cable at the front derailleur.

Top right: Fig. 14.24. View of front derailleur, showing the screw that can be removed to release the chain.

Bottom right: Fig. 14.25. Tightening or loosening the front derailleur mounting bolt.

Replace Front Derailleur

Front derailleurs are either mounted with a clamp that fits around the seat tube or directly on a tab that's welded to the seat tube. Either way, they'll be held with an Allan bolt on modern bikes, while on older bikes it may be a conventional hexagonal-head bolt and nut.

Tools and equipment:

- Allan wrenches (or whatever kind of wrenches fit)

- screwdriver to open up the derailleur cage to remove the chain

Removal Procedure:

1. Remove the little screw that holds the two sides of the derailleur cage together so you can remove the chain (or, if it cannot easily be opened, disconnect the chain, following the instructions in Chapter 13).

2. Undo the cable.

3. Remove the mounting bolt and remove the derailleur.

Installation Procedure:

1. Place the mounting bolt on the derailleur eye or the mounting plate and thread it in about 1½ turns by hand.

2. Swivel the derailleur back against the spring tension until it passes the prong on the derailleur eye or the mounting plate; then screw the bolt in further with the wrench.

3. Open up the cage and remove the jockey pulley.

4. Feed the chain through and reinstall the jockey pulley, holding back the derailleur cage against its spring tension.

Above: Fig. 14.27. Integrated brake-shift device on a road bike, here with the brake lever pulled to reveal its interior.

Below: Fig. 14.28. Attachment of twist-grip type shifter.

5. Place the chain on the appropriate cog and chainring.

6. Attach the cable.

7. Check operation of the gears and make any adjustments necessary, following the procedure above.

Above: Fig. 14.29. Handlebar-end ("bar-con") shifter.

Below: Fig. 14.30. Downtube shifter removed to show cable routing.

Left: Fig. 14.26. Shifter on bike with flat handlebars.

Shifter Maintenance

There's not much you can do on modern integrated shifters: they either work or they have to be replaced in their entirety. If your bike is equipped with separately mounted shifters, you can simply take them apart and see whether there's something damaged or, more typically, loose, dirty, or corroded. Fix what you find to be wrong and tighten the bolt that holds everything together when done. Adjust the relevant derailleur after such work, and chances are you've taken care of the problem. If not, you'll just have to replace the entire shifter.

Freewheel and Cogs

The rear wheel cogs are mounted on a freewheel mechanism, which contains a kind of ratcheting system to turn forward when driven by the rider without forcing the rider to be pedaling forward all the time.

The freewheel is either integrated into a portion of the hub (in the case of the modern so-called cassette hub) or in a separate unit that is screwed on to the hub (in the case of the older freewheel block). The various cogs are either screwed on or held on splines and held together with a screwed-on item (either a separate lock ring or the smallest cog).

At least once a year, clean the cogs — and the spaces between them. To clean between the cogs, use a thin cloth folded into a narrow strip, stretched between both hands, going back and forth all around (it's easiest with the wheel removed off the bike). If dirt doesn't come off, soak the cloth in a mixture of solvent and 5–10% mineral oil.

Individual cogs can be replaced by first removing the last, screwed-on item. This is done with a special tool — buy the appropriate tool for the type of freewheel on your bike if you want to do this work yourself. Especially on modern cassette hubs, the choice of cogs is rather limited, in that they come in sets, and usually it will not be

possible to pick different sequences of cogs, as can be done with the old-fashioned screwed-on freewheel block.

When replacing an entire cassette — or some of the cogs on a cassette — make sure they are compatible. I also suggest replacing the chain at that time, ascertaining at the bike shop that it is suitable for the particular cassette.

One reason you might want to replace one or more of the cogs would be in case of wear, when the chain starts to skip. At that point, you should replace both the cog in question (usually the smallest one) *and* the chain, because the old, "stretched" chain would not fit the tooth pattern on the new cog.

The freewheel body can be lubricated with thick

Fig. 14.31. Cleaning behind and between the cogs.

Fig. 14.32. Lubricating cassette freewheel using Morningstar's "Freehub buddy" tool

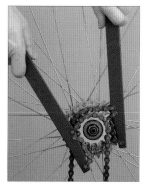

Fig. 14.33. Separating cogs from a screwed-on freewheel.

Fig. 14.34. Inserting freewheel tool to disassemble cassette cogs.

Fig. 14.36. Smallest cog removed from cassette.

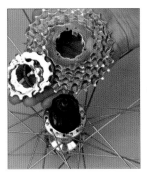

Fig. 14.37. Disassembly of cassette cogs.

Fig. 14.38. Removing freewheel mechanism from cassette hub.

Fig. 14.35. Using freewheel tool to disassemble cassette cogs. Hold the cog set with a chain whip to stop it from rotating.

mineral oil (SAE 60) inserted in the visible gap between moving parts inside.

If the freewheel mechanism fails or becomes either too loose or too rough, it can be replaced, for which the old one has to be removed from the hub. The screwed-on type is removed with a special freewheel tool: remove the wheel, hold the tool loosely with the wheel's quick-release skewer, then unscrew it, using a large wrench, holding the wheel firmly (loosen the quick-release thumb nut as needed along the way). The cassette freewheel can be removed with a 10 mm Allan wrench as shown in Fig. 14.38. If it's a screwed-

on type, clean and lubricate the screw thread, and screw the new freewheel on by hand. If it's a cassette, it is held on by means of a hollow internal 10 mm Allan bolt, accessible after you remove the axle.

When a spoke on the chain side of the rear wheel breaks, you have to remove the freewheel (in the case of a screwed-on freewheel block) or the cogs (in the case of a cassette hub). This is probably the most common reason to remove these items.

Adapt Gear Range

If the gears on your bike are not high enough or, more typically, not low enough, you can change that by replacing chainrings or cogs by bigger or

smaller ones. To achieve a higher top gear, you could exchange either the smallest cog by a smaller one or the largest chainring by a larger one. To achieve a lower low gear, replace either the biggest cog by a bigger one or the smallest chainring by a smaller one.

That's the theory. In practice, these days, cogs and chainrings usually come "prepackaged" in certain combinations, and it may be hard or impossible to find a single replacement cog or chainring to match your needs. Find out at the bike shop which combinations are available to satisfy your needs and exchange them accordingly — whether individually or as set of several matching ones.

To exchange chainrings, first select a low gear, and lift the chain off the chainring. Then undo the little bolts that hold the chainrings to the right-hand crank. Install the new chainring(s) with the same bolts and replace the chain.

To exchange cogs, first remove the rear wheel. Then either unscrew the smallest cog that holds the rest together on a cassette hub, or use the chain whip to separate the cogs on a screwed-on freewheel. Put the new cog(s) in place and reinstall the wheel. If you installed larger cogs or chainrings, you may need a wide-range derailleur and a longer chain to accommodate them.

CHAPTER 15

Hub Gearing Maintenance

This chapter addresses the most common maintenance aspects of hub gears. Although it's usually looked down upon, hub gearing is only marginally less efficient than derailleur gearing, and it does offer some practical advantages.

With the mechanism hidden inside the wheel hub, it's less sensitive to damage and the ravages of the weather, which makes it a good choice in areas where people actually use their bikes for everyday transportation. It's also easier to

Fig. 15.1. Hub gear drivetrain.

use, trading the many options available on a derailleur system for fewer, but more easily selected gears.

In addition to straightforward hub gearing, it's also possible to use a hybrid system. In this case, a hub gear is used in combination with a rear derailleur. Another hybrid option, though not strictly a hub gear, is the Mountain Drive 2-speed gear built into a crankset, which also replaces the front derailleur. Hybrid systems lend themselves well for use on folding and recumbent bicycles.

The major manufacturers of hub gearing are Shimano, SRAM (after they took over Sachs), and Sturmey-Archer (which is now just a brand name owned by Sun Race). All three major manufacturers have in recent years done

much to widen the range of available gears on their hub gearing systems.

Hub Gearing Components

A straightforward hub gearing system consists of a gear mechanism contained in a special hub in the rear wheel, a shifter mounted on the handlebars, and a control cable. The hub may offer anywhere from 2 to 7 different gearing stages (although Rohloff makes a fine, and expensive, 14-speed hub).

The gear hub contains one or more planetary drive systems that are too complex to describe here. However, their function is straightforward: depending on the gear selected, their single cog turns faster or slower than the hub, and

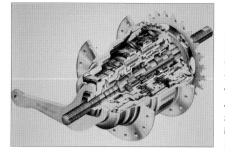

Fig. 15.2. Manufacturer's illustration of the workings of a modern seven-speed hub gear (Shimano).

Right: Fig. 15.3. Control mechanism at Shimano seven-speed hub gear.

hence the wheel itself. When the wheel turns slower than the cog, you're in a low gear; when both turn at the same speed, you've got the "normal" gear; and when the wheel turns faster than the cog, you're in a high gear.

The shifter is either in the form of a lever (or even two separate levers) mounted on the handlebars, or in the form of a twist grip or twist ring mounted instead of or inboard from the handgrip on the handlebars.

The control cable connects the shifter with a selector mechanism on the side of the hub (usually on the right, but it can be either side, or even on both sides).

Although hybrid gearing systems use a freewheel cassette with several cogs on the rear wheel, normal hub gears

come with a single cog, which is held on to the hub with splines and a spring clip. Removing the spring clip allows you to replace the cog.

The gear hub is often combined with a brake. That may be either a coaster brake, a drum brake, or a roller brake. Operation of the coaster brake is by pedaling back, while drum and roller brakes are controlled by a brake lever on the handlebars via a cable. If you have to remove such a wheel from the bike for maintenance, you'll have to disconnect the brake counter lever and the brake control cable as well as the gear control cable itself — and install and adjust them again afterwards.

Hub Gear Maintenance

If bought new, these hubs come with an instruction manual that deals with basic handling and adjusting. If you got one, refer to it, because the instructions there will be more specific to the make and model in question. If not, here are some tips to help you on your way.

When a hub gearing system does not work properly, it's usually something that can be alleviated with adjusting. If that doesn't do the job, you may well be faced with having to replace one of the system components — the shifter, the control cable, or the hub itself. Keeping the components clean and lightly lubricated is your major line of defense against hub gear trouble.

Gear malfunctions usually show up as failure to shift into a specific gear properly; sometimes none of the gears can be engaged, with the chain apparently slipping.

The first thing to try, of course, is simple adjusting. All hub gear systems come with an

Above: Fig. 15.6. Adjusting detail at SRAM hub gear "click-box" device.

Below: Fig. 15.7. On older hubs, and even today on most three-speeds, this rod with attached chain controls the operation of the gears.

Fig. 15. 4. Matching up the color-coded marks on a Shimano seven-speed hub gear.

Fig. 15.5. On Sturmey-Archer three-speed hubs, the gears are adjusted, and the cable connected, at this barrel adjuster.

adjusting device either at the shifter or at the hub.

Hub Gear Adjustment

Tools and equipment:

• Usually none required

Procedure:

1. Set the shifter for the highest gear, while rotating the cranks from the pedal by hand with the rear wheel off the ground.

2. Check the cable where it attaches to

Fig. 15.9. Adjusting gears at the shifter on a modern Shimano twist-grip shifter.

the control mechanism at the hub: in the selected position, the cable should be just slack, i.e., without tension. However, as soon as you shift down, the cable should become taut and the hub should engage the next gear as you move it to the next setting at the shifter.

3. If it doesn't shift properly, turn the adjuster in (to loosen) half a turn at a time and check whether the situation improves. If not, loosen

Fig. 15.8. Adjusting Sturmey-Archer 3-speed hub.

Fig. 15.10. Shift-lever type control for 3-speed hub.

it in similar increments.

SRAM note:

These hubs (and their Sachs predecessors) are equipped with an ingenious adjuster. Instead of a conventional adjusting barrel, there is a little metal or plastic bracket with a spring clip, into which the threaded adjusting pin is pushed and held in place. Easy to connect, to disconnect, and to adjust: just push the clip while pulling the threaded pin all the way out, then insert the pin again until the cable tension is right.

General note:

Sometimes the control that projects from the hub, which is in the form of a little chain (especially on older hubs) is either too loose or turned in un-

der such an angle that the little chain is kinked. In the first case, undo the connection with the cable, and screw the control into the hub a little tighter; then reattach. In the second case, undo and loosen it a little so it is not kinked; then reattach.

Additional Maintenance Suggestions

If the problem can't be alleviated with simple adjusting as described

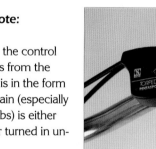

Fig. 15.11. Older shift-lever type control for 2-cable 5-speed hub.

Fig. 15.12. SRAM twist-grip type shifter.

Fig. 15.13. Seven-speed lever-type shifter disassembled.

Fig. 15.14. Attachment detail of twist-grip type shifter.

Fig. 15.15. Replacing cog on hub gear to adapt the gearing range.

above, see what you can do with the following suggestions:

1. Clean and lightly lubricate all parts first — hub, cog(s), chain, control mechanism, cable, and shifter.

2. Check whether it's really is a malfunction in the system itself (although that usually is the cause, you don't want to be barking up the wrong tree if it isn't): make sure the chain is properly tensioned, the wheel properly positioned, and the chainring and cog(s) engage the chain properly.

3. Next, check to make sure the cable is in good condition; free

it if it is caught somewhere along the way, lubricate it if it is dry, and replace it if it is kinked or frayed.

4. Loosen the control cable, and check whether the shifter works smoothly when it is not attached to the hub. If it doesn't, see what you can do to make it work, or replace it with a new one.

5. If the problem does not get resolved this way, it's time to take the bike to a bike shop that has information on hub gears (at least in the US, these things are still too rare for every bike shop to be equipped for them — and even if they are, they may suggest

just replacing instead of repairing).

Adjust Gear Range

The gearing range with which the hub-geared bike comes may not be to your liking. Often the gearing range is either too high or too low. In theory, you can make all the gears lower or higher by replacing either the chainring or the cog by one of a different size. In practice, it'll be hard to replace the chainring. So to get higher gears, install a smaller cog. To get lower gears, install a larger cog (and adjusting the rear wheel position or chain length to match).

To replace the cog, remove the rear wheel, pry the spring clip out of its groove with a small screwdriver, and then lift

out the cog, replace it with another one for that make and model of hub, and push the spring clip back into place. When working on the spring clip, hold it down with a cloth so it does not accidentally "jump" out at you.

If you're unhappy with the "width" of the gearing range, e.g., you find that the low gear is not low enough *and* the high gear not high enough, you don't have much choice — at best, you may be able to replace a 3-speed by a 7-speed, which does have a wider range (but that means a new hub, a rebuilt wheel, and a new shifter — difficult and expensive). So if you're really picky about your gears, only a derailleur system will offer the flexibility you're looking for.

CHAPTER 16

Handlebar Maintenance

There are two distinct handlebar types: "drop" handlebars, for use on road bikes, and flat bars, for use on mountain bikes and most other bicycle types.

The handlebars themselves are usually connected to the bike's steering system, consisting of front fork and headset bearings, via a stem that is clamped to the front fork's steerer tube and around the center portion of the handlebars.

After the brake levers are installed on the bars, the drop bars get wrapped with handlebar tapes, while flat bars get equipped with handgrips pushed on at the ends.

The handlebars are held in the stem by means of a clamp integrated in the stem that is held by means of one or two Allan bolts. How the stem attaches to the fork's steerer tube depends on the type of headset used on the bike in question (see Chapter 17).

On bikes with a conventional threaded headset, the stem is held in the fork's steerer tube by means of a wedge (or sometimes a conical item) that in turn is clamped in with a binder bolt reached from the top of the stem. On bikes with a threadless headset, the stem is clamped around an extension of the fork's steerer tube that sticks out above the upper headset.

Adjust Handlebar Height

This simplest of all handlebar adaptations only works on bikes with a conventional threaded headset (on bikes with a threadless headset, the only way to raise or lower the handlebars is by means of installing a different stem).

Tools and equipment:

- Allan wrench (or, for older low-end bikes, regular wrench)
- mallet (or a hammer and a protective block of wood)

Procedure:

1. Clamp the front wheel between your legs from the front and loosen the binder bolt on top of the stem by about 5 turns.

Fig. 16.3. Handlebar height adjustment this way is only possible on bikes with a conventional threaded headset.

Fig. 16.1. Flat handlebars with conventional threaded headset.

Fig. 16.2. Flat handlebars with threadless headset.

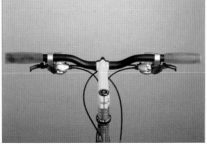

2. Tap on the bolt with a mallet (or a hammer, protecting the bolt with a block of wood) to loosen the wedge inside the stem — the bolt will drop down, loosening the stem.

3. Raise or lower the handlebars as desired and hold them there firmly.

4. Check to make sure the marking that shows the maximum extension of the stem does not show above the headset (and if it does, lower the stem until it doesn't, be-cause raising it too high might cause it to break or come loose).

5. Holding the handle-bars at the desired

Fig. 16.4. Handlebar angle adjustment is done with this binder bolt.

height and straight (still clamping the front wheel between your legs), tighten the bolt on top of the stem firmly.

Note:

*   At least 2½ inches (6.5 cm) of the stem must remain clamped in. Usually, the stem is marked for this inser-tion depth, but even if it's not, that's the mini-mum for safety.

Adjust Handlebar Angle

Especially for drop han-dlebars, this adjustment

Fig. 16.5. Handlebar clamping detail with conventional threaded headset. This one has a cone-shaped clamp, whereas wedge-shaped clamps are now more common.

allows you to find a more comfortable rotation of the handlebars, if needed.

Tools and equipment:

*   Allan wrench (or for older models, regular wrench)

Procedure:

1. Undo the clamp bolt(s) that hold the stem clamp around the handlebars by about one turn.

2. Turn the handlebars into the desired orien-tation, making sure they remain centered on the stem.

3. Holding the bars in the desired orientation and location, tighten the stem clamp bolt(s).

Replace Handlebars

Do this work if the handle-bars are damaged in a fall

or simply because you want to try a different type. Before proceeding, make sure the new han-dlebars actually fit the stem that's installed on the bike (or replace the stem as well — see the description *Replace Stem* below).

Tools and equipment:

*   Allan wrench (or, for older low-end bikes, regular wrench) and whatever tools are needed to remove items installed on the handlebars.

Procedure:

1. Remove anything in-stalled on the handle-bars (such as brake levers, gear shifters, handgrips or handle-bar tape, etc.).

2. Unscrew the bolt(s) that hold the clamp on the stem around the center section of the handlebars.

Right:
Fig. 16.6. Handlebar binder bolts removed on threadless headset type handlebars.

3. Pull the handlebars out, wiggling and rotating them until they come out. (You may have to pry open the clamp with the aid of a large screwdriver to get enough clearance.)

4. Tighten the clamp bolt(s) when the handlebars are in the right location and orientation.

5. Reinstall all items that were removed in Step 1 above.

Replace Stem

This operation may be needed if the stem that's on the bike brings the handlebars too far forward or not far enough, or — especially in combination with a threadless headset — too low or too high. If it's too long, you want one with less "reach"; if it's too low, one with "more rise." Make sure you get a replacement stem of the same general type (i.e., for the same type and size of steerer tube and the same diameter handlebars). You'll also have to remove the handlebars from the stem and reinstall them when you've finished, following the procedure *Replace Handlebars* above.

Tools and equipment:

- Allan wrenches (or, for older low-end bikes, regular wrench)

- mallet (or a hammer and a protective block of wood)

- for threaded headset: cloth and lubricant

Procedure:

1. Establish whether this is a bike with a threaded or threadless headset (compare the illustrations).

   - On a threaded headset, undo the bolt on top of the stem by about 5 turns and then tap on the bolt with a mallet (or a hammer and a protective block of wood) to loosen the stem.

   - On a threadless headset, first undo the Allan bolt on the top of the stem (which is only an adjusting bolt), then remove this bolt and the underlying plastic cap, and finally loosen the clamp bolts that clamp the stem around the fork's steerer tube extension that sticks out above the upper headset bearing.

3. Remove the old stem.

4. Open the bolts on the new stem (if it's for a threaded headset: far enough so the wedge is loose enough to line up perfectly with the stem without touching it).

   - On a threaded headset, place the new stem in place (first put some lubricant on the screw-threaded portion of the bolt and the wedge or cone), and orient it properly.

   - On a threadless headset, put the stem in place, after installing any spacers required; but

Fig. 16.7. Loosening or tightening the adjustment screw on threadless headset type handlebars.

Fig. 16.8. Loosening or tightening the stem clamp bolts on a threadless headset.

Right: Fig. 16.9. Replacing handgrips on flat handlebars.

don't tighten the bolts that clamp it around the fork's smooth steerer tube extension yet. Install the cap and the bolt on top, and use the bolt to adjust the headset (refer to Chapter 17 for instructions), and only then tighten those clamp bolts.

6. While firmly holding the handlebars in place, tighten the bolt(s).

7. After you've installed the handlebars, make any final adjustments necessary.

Fig. 16.10. Installing handlebar extensions for mountain bike use.

Replace Handgrips on Flat Handlebars

Do this if the old grips are not comfortable — or if you have to replace the brake lever, the gear shifter, or the handlebars or the stem.

Tools and equipment:

- screwdriver

- sometimes hot water, dishwashing liquid, hair spray, knife

Procedure:

1. Remove the old handgrips by pulling and twisting — if they do not come off easily, place the screw-

Fig. 16.11. Replacing handlebar tape, shown here with the integrated brake-shift-device removed. First tape down any cable that's routed along the handlebars.

driver under the old grip and let some dishwashing liquid enter between the grip and the handlebars. If all else fails, cut the grip lengthwise and "peel" it off.

2. Push the new handgrips over the ends of the handlebars. If they don't go on easily, soak them in warm water first. To make them adhere better, you can spray some hair spray inside the grips just before installing them.

Install Bar Ends on Flat Handlebars

Bar ends are forward pointing extensions that can be installed at the

Fig. 16.12. Cover the brake lever mounting strap with a single piece of tape.

ends of flat mountain bike handlebars to offer the rider an additional, for some more comfortable, riding position. They're clamped around the ends of the handlebars. Since these things may form a potential hazard in a fall if they stick straight out, look for a model that curves in and has flexible protection at the ends.

Tools and equipment:

- Allan wrench

Procedure:

1. Remove the existing handgrips, and replace them with open-ended grips, pushed about ¾ inch (2 cm) further to the center of the bars. (Alternately, you can cut the ends off the existing ones and slide them in that far).

Fig. 16.13. Taping around the brake lever mount.

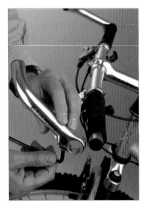
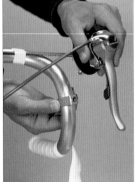

Above: Fig. 16.14.
Working toward the middle of the handlebars, covering any control cable that's routed along the handlebars.

Below: Fig. 16.15. Covering the ends with a short piece of adhesive tape.

Below: Fig. 16.16. Installing handlebar end plug, or cap.

2. Place the bar ends over the uncovered ends of the handlebars, with the clamping bolts underneath — the extensions pointing forward and slightly up (by about 15 degrees).

3. Tighten the clamp bolts very firmly, while making sure both point up under the same angle.

4. Ride the bike and do any fine-tuning that may be necessary.

Replace Handlebar Tape on Drop Handlebars

Replace the tape used on road bike handlebars when it becomes tattered or uncomfortable — and when you need to replace either the bars themselves, the stem, or one of the items installed on the handlebars. If available, choose a type of tape that is thicker in the middle than at the sides. If it has adhesive backing, it should only be in the middle portion.

Tools and equipment:

• screwdriver (for some bar-end plugs)

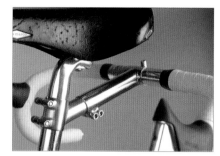

Fig. 16.17. Special rear handlebar stem on a tandem, clamped to the front rider's seat post.

• knife or scissors

Procedure:

1. If the plugs have screws in the end, loosen the screws about 5 turns and remove the plugs by pulling and twisting.

   • If there are no screws, just pry them off.

2. Cut the tape at the end closest to the center of the bars and unwind the tape from the bars. At the brake levers, lift the rubber hoods far enough to get access to all the tape.

3. Make sure the brake levers are symmetrically mounted where they are comfortable to reach when riding.

4. If necessary, tape down the brake cable (and sometimes, e.g., on touring bikes with handlebar-end shifters, the derailleur cable) at 4-inch (10 cm) intervals.

5. Place a 4-inch (10 cm) section of tape across the brake lever mounting strap.

6. Starting at the ends, where you tuck in the first inch of tape, wrap the bars inward, overlapping each subsequent layer half-way with the next layer.

7. Cross-wrap at the brake levers and continue straight to a point about 3 inches (about 7.5 cm) from the center.

8. Reinstall the bar-end plugs.

9. Wrap a 4-inch (10 cm) long piece of adhesive tape around the ends of the taped sections.

117

CHAPTER 17

Headset Maintenance

The headset is what supports the bike's steering system. It consists of an upper and a lower set of ball bearings, mounted in the top and the bottom of the frame's head tube, respectively.

Unlike other bearings on the bike, they get most of their work without rotating much — from road shocks parallel to their axis. Therefore at least the lower bearing must be a so-called axial bearing (as opposed to the regular radial bear-ings used elsewhere on the bike).

Two different types of headset are in common use on modern bikes. The conventional bearing has a screw-threaded adjustable bearing race that is screwed onto the fork's steerer tube. The currently favored headset for mountain bike use is the threadless type, which is adjusted from the top of the handlebar stem. There us also something called an integrated headset, which is similar to the thread-less bearing but consists of fewer parts, sitting directly in the frame's head tube. Comparing the illustrations will help you define which type is installed on the bike you're working on.

Maintenance work on the headset includes adjusting, overhauling, and replacing the bearings. These operations are different for the two major types of headset. Some of this work also has to be carried out when you have to replace e.g., the front fork.

Adjust Conventional Threaded Headset

If the bearings are too tight or too loose, first try whether adjusting will solve the problem. If not, you'll have to proceed to the instructions for over-hauling, or even replacing, the headset.

Tools and equipment:

- headset wrenches (make sure they're the size to match the make and model in question)

- sometimes a large adjustable wrench can be used as a substitute for a specific size headset wrench)

- sometimes a tiny Allan wrench, if there's a grub screw to hold down the bearing locknut

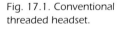

Fig. 17.1. Conventional threaded headset.

Fig. 17.2. Threadless headset.

Right: Fig. 17.3. Adjusting threaded headset bearings.

Procedure:

1. Loosen the locknut on top of the upper headset bearing about one turn (unless there is a toothed ring underneath, on some older headsets — in that case far enough to free those teeth). If the locknut is held with a grub screw, loosen that little screw before trying to undo the locknut.

2. Lift the keyed washer that lies under the locknut to allow the adjustable bearing race to be rotated.

3. Turn the adjustable bearing face in 1/8-turn increments (clockwise to tighten, counterclockwise to loosen) until it feels just barely loose (that slack will get taken up when the locknut is screwed down).

4. Tighten the locknut fully, while holding the adjustable race with the other wrench.

5. Check to make sure the bearing is properly adjusted now, or fine-tune the adjustment, if necessary, then tighten the locknut firmly.

Adjust Threadless Headset

The threadless headset tends to stay properly adjusted longer, but there may still be a need for adjustment from time to time.

Tools and equipment:

- Allan wrenches

Procedure:

1. Loosen the clamp bolts that hold the stem around the fork's steerer tube by about one turn each.

2. Tighten or loosen the Allan bolt on top of the stem — this is not a binder bolt taking force but solely serves as an adjustment bolt (and the plastic or aluminum cap underneath would break if too much force were applied to it by that bolt). Tighten by turning the bolt clockwise, loosen by turning it counterclockwise.

3. When the adjustment feels right, tighten the stem clamp bolts, making sure the handlebars are straight.

Overhaul or Replace Conventional Threaded Headset

Do this work when the steering has become rough and the problem cannot be solved by simply adjusting the headset bearings in accordance with the preceding instructions. Before starting, remove the handlebar stem from the bike, following the procedure in Chapter 16. Also remove the front wheel and unhook the front brake cable.

Tools and equipment:

- headset wrenches or substitute wrenches

- sometimes a tiny Allan wrench if there's a grub screw to hold down the bearing locknut

- cloth

- bearing grease

Disassembly procedure:

1. Loosen and remove the locknut on top of the upper headset (if appropriate, after unscrewing a grub screw that may be present on some models).

Fig. 17.4. On some threaded headsets, there's a grub screw that must be loosened before you can undo the locknut.

Fig. 17.5. Loosening or tightening the bolt on a threadless headset. To adjust the bearing, this bolt is also used, but **after** the stem binder bolts have been loosened.

2. Lift and remove the keyed washer from the fork's screw-threaded steerer tube (note that the steerer tube has a matching groove or flat spot cut into the screw thread) — that's to stop the washer from rotating.

3. Unscrew the adjustable bearing race (if necessary, after loosening a grub screw) while holding the fork and the frame together at the fork crown.

4. Remove the bearing balls from the upper fixed bearing race (usually held in a retainer).

Fig. 17.6. Loosening or tightening the stem binder bolts on a threadless headset.

5. Pull the fork out of the frame, catching the bearing balls (usually also in a retainer) from the lower headset bearing.

Overhauling procedure:

1. Clean and inspect all parts, replacing any parts that are damaged, corroded, pitted, or grooved. A particular problem to watch for is "brinelling" of a bearing surface, i.e., pitting caused by repeated impact at the same point (most prevalent at the lower headset bearing).

   • When replacing parts (or, for that matter, when replacing an entire headset) be aware that they come in different sizes — take the fork with you to the shop to get one that's guaranteed to fit.

2. If the entire headset has to be replaced, it will be best to have a bike shop remove and install the fixed components (the upper and lower cups on the head tube and

the fork race on the fork crown), because those jobs are best done with special tools.

Installation procedure:

1. Fill the upper and lower fixed bearing races with bearing grease.

2. Holding the frame upside down, put the bearing balls (usually in a retainer) in the lower fixed race.

3. Holding the fork upside down as well, push the fork's steerer tube through until the bearing balls of the lower headset bearing are securely held between the fork

Fig. 17.7. Keyed washer on a threaded headset.

race and the lower fixed race.

4. Turn the bike the right way round, carefully holding the fork crown and the lower part of the head tube together.

5. Still holding things together with one hand, put the bearing balls (also usually in a retainer) into the upper fixed bearing race, then screw the adjustable bearing race onto the fork's steerer tube until the bearing is just a tad loose.

6. Install the keyed washer on the adjustable bearing race, matching the prong or the flat part of the

Fig. 17.8. Bearing ball retainer.

washer up with the groove or flat area on the threaded portion of the steerer tube. Also install any other items that may have to go between the lock washer and the locknut (e.g., spacer, cantilever brake stop, or reflector mounting bracket).

7. Holding the adjustable bearing cup with one tool, install and tighten the locknut fully.

8. Check whether the headset is now adjusted properly (i.e., free to rotate without resistance on the one hand or looseness — or "play"— on the other, and fine-tune

Fig. 17.9. The fork race and bearings, i.e., the parts of the lower headset bearing.

the adjustment, if necessary.

Note regarding cartridge bearings:

Some conventional-looking headsets on high-end bikes may come with cartridge bearings. No adjustment possible, and you'll have to get them replaced at a bike shop if they should give you trouble after long, hard use.

Overhaul or Replace Threadless Headset

The threadless headset rarely needs maintenance work, but if it does give you trouble, you can take it apart and/or replace it. The most important things to be aware of is that it requires a special fork that does not have screw thread on the steerer tube, and that the bolt on top of the stem does not hold the parts together but is merely there for adjustment. Before you start, remove the front wheel and unhook the front brake cable.

Tools and equipment:

• Allan wrenches
• cloth
• bearing grease

Disassembly procedure:

1. Undo the Allan bolt on top of the stem and remove it, together with the underlying cap.

2. Holding the fork and the bottom of the head tube together, loosen the bolts that clamp the stem around the top portion of the fork's steerer tube; then remove the stem.

Fig. 17.10. Removing the cap from the top of a threadless headset.

3. Pull the fork out of the head tube, catching the bearing balls.

Overhauling procedure:

1. Clean and inspect all parts, replacing any parts that are damaged, corroded, pitted, or grooved. A particular problem to watch for is "brinelling" of a bearing surface, which means pitting caused by repeated impact at the same point (most prevalent at the lower headset bearing). When replacing parts (or, for that matter, when replacing an entire headset) be aware that they come in different sizes — take the fork with you

Fig. 17.11. View showing what the manufacturer calls the "star-fangled nut," into which the bolt on top engages for bearing adjustment of a threadless headset.

121

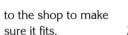

Fig. 17.12. The stem removed from the threadless headset. The spacers help get the desired handlebar height.

Fig. 17.13. The fork race on a threadless headset exposed. The bearing assembly itself sits at the bottom of the head tube.

to the shop to make sure it fits.

2. In case the entire headset has to be re-placed, it will be best to have a bike shop remove and install the fixed compo-nents (fixed upper and lower cups on the head tube and fork race on the fork crown), because that job is best done with special tools.

Installation procedure:

1. Fill the upper and lower fixed bearing races with bearing grease.

2. Holding the frame upside down, put the bearing balls (usually in a retainer) in the lower fixed race.

3. Holding the fork up-side down as well, push the fork's steerer tube through until the bearing balls of the lower headset bearing are securely held between the fork race and the lower fixed race.

4. Turn the bike the right way round, carefully holding the fork and the lower part of the head tube together.

5. Still holding things together with one hand, first put the bearing balls (also usually in a retainer) into the upper fixed bearing race and then slide the adjust-able bearing race onto the fork's steerer tube.

6. Install the slotted ta-pered ring (or two ta-pered segments) in the gap, and place the washer on top — followed by any other spacers that may be needed, then slide the stem on and pro-visionally screw the stem clamp bolts just enough to hold things together but free to slide.

7. Install the cap on top of the stem and at-tach it loosely with the Allan bolt on top, screwing the latter into what the manu-facturer refers to as a "star-fangled" nut in-side the fork's steerer tube.

8. Adjust the bearing with the Allan bolt on top of the stem (clockwise to tighten,

counterclockwise to loosen the bearing), then tighten the stem clamp bolts with the handlebars in the correct orientation.

Note:

• If the "star-fangled" nut is pushed too far into the steerer tube, or if it goes under an angle, you can push it out from the bottom (holding the fork up-side-down) with a large screwdriver and a hammer or a mallet. Then have a bike shop push it (or a replace-ment) in again from the top, using a spe-cial tool.

Integrated Headset Note:

Integrated headsets work just like the threadless headset, except that the bearing races are perma-nently integrated with the head tube and the parts just slide into place. Adjustment, re-moval, overhaul, and in-stallation follow the same procedure, as adapted for the fewer parts that are actually there.

CHAPTER 18

Saddle Maintenance

The saddle, or seat, is usually made of a firm but flexible plastic base, held on a metal frame, with a real or simulated leather cover over a thin layer of soft padding.

Racing saddles are narrow and firm, while saddles intended for an upright riding position tend to be wide and soft (or rather: not quite so rock hard). Some saddles are made of self-supporting thick and firm leather, directly connected to the metal frame.

The saddle is held on the bike by means of a tubular seatpost, which is clamped in at the seat lug, at the top of the frame's seat tube. Different inside diameters of seat tube call for seatposts with (slightly) different outside diameters. The seat lug is split in the back and tightened around the seatpost with a clamp, which is either bolted together or clamped with a quick-release.

Adjust Saddle Height

Once you've determined how high you want the saddle to be, this is how you get it there.

Tools and equipment:

- Depending on the type of clamp, either none (if quick-release) or Allan wrench (modern quality bike), or regular wrench (older or low-end bike)

Procedure:

1. Depending on the type of saddle clamp:

   - On a bike with a regular bolted clamp, undo the bolt (referred to as binder bolt) by 2–3 turns.

   - On a bike with quick-release clamp, twist the quick-release lever into the "open" position.

Fig. 18.1. Saddle and seatpost on a high-end hybrid.

Fig. 18.2. Adjusting the saddle height.

Fig. 18.3. Adjusting saddle height on a bike with a quick-release binder bolt.

Fig. 18.4. Saddle attachment detail — use the bolt(s) under the saddle to adjust the saddle angle or its forward position.

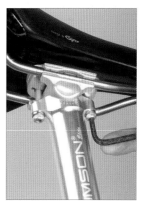

2. Try to move the seatpost up or down in a twisting movement, using the saddle for leverage and holding the bike's frame. If it doesn't budge, squirt some penetrating oil in at the point where the seat lug is slotted, so it enters between the seatpost and the seat tube. Wait 2–3 minutes and try again.

3. Move it to the exact location where you want it to be, but make sure the marker that shows the minimum insertion depth is not exposed (if it is, it'll be dangerous to ride that way, and you'll need either a longer seatpost or a bigger frame).

4. Holding the saddle at the right height and straight ahead, tighten the binder bolt or the quick-release. (If the quick-release can't be

tightened properly, flip it to "open" again, adjust the thumb nut on the other side, and try again.)

5. Check to make sure the position is correct, and fine-tune the various adjustments, if necessary.

   • You may find that you now need to adjust the angle and forward position in accordance with the instructions below as well.

Note:

• At least 2½ inches (6.5 cm) of the seatpost must be clamped in. Usually the seatpost is marked to show this minimum safe insertion depth.

Adjust Saddle Angle and Forward Position

These features are adjusted by means of one or more bolts, usually accessible from underneath the saddle, that hold the saddle wires to the seatpost.

Tools and equipment:

• Allan wrench (or sometimes a regular wrench for an older bike)

Procedure:

1. Look under the saddle and identify the bolts in question; usually they're easily accessible from below, but they can be tricky to get at on old saddles (between the saddle cover and the clamp); and on low-end bikes there's one nut on ei-

ther side of the wires (or the flat rails often used on such saddles).

2. Loosen the bolts (usually there are two) or the one bolt (if there is only one) about 3 turns.

3. Move the saddle forward or backward on the wires (while making sure the clamp does not run off those wires) and hold it at the desired location under the desired angle.

5. Holding the saddle steadily in place, tighten the bolts —

Fig. 18.7. On bikes with sprung saddles, you may find this kind of saddle attachment with a separate clip and a tubular seatpost. You can reverse the clip to move the saddle further back.

Fig. 18.6. Seatpost clamp disassembled.

Left:
Fig. 18.5. Adjusting the saddle angle on a seatpost clamp with a single bolt.

gradually tightening both of them in turn if there are two.

6. Check to make sure the position is correct, and fine-tune the various adjustments, if necessary (it may also have affected the height adjustment).

Replace Saddle

To do this work, e.g., because you want to try a more comfortable model, you can either leave the seatpost clamped in at the bike or you can work on it while it's off the bike.

Fig. 18.8. The seatpost must be clamped in by at least 2½ inches (65 mm) and is usually marked for this minimal safe insertion depth.

Tools and equipment:

- Allan wrench (or sometimes a regular wrench on an older bike)

Procedure:

1. Look under the saddle and identify the bolts in question; usually they're easily accessible from below, but they can be tricky to get at on old saddles.

2. Loosen the bolt or bolts (usually there are two) far enough to twist the saddle off the clip.

3. Install the new saddle on the clamp and hold it loosely with the bolts or nuts.

4. Move the saddle forward or backward on

Fig. 18.9. Replacing the saddle on the seatpost clip.

the wires (while making sure the clamp does not run off those wires) and hold it at the desired location under the desired angle.

5. Holding the saddle steadily in place, tighten the bolts — gradually tightening both of them in turn if there are two.

6. Check to make sure the position is correct, and fine-tune the various adjustments, if necessary.

Replace Seatpost

To remove the seatpost, first leave the saddle on the seatpost and remove the two together as a single unit, then take the seatpost off the saddle.

Tools and equipment:

- Depending on the type of clamp, either none (if

Right: Fig. 18.10. Adjusting the tension of a leather saddle cover.

quick-release), an Allan wrench, or a regular wrench (older or low-end bike)

- cloth
- grease
- sometimes penetrating oil

Procedure:

1. Depending on the type of clamp:

  - On a bike with a regular bolted clamp, undo the binder bolt 2–3 turns.

  - On a bike with a quick-release clamp, twist the quick-release lever into the "open" position.

2. Try to move the seatpost up in a twisting movement, using the saddle for leverage. If it doesn't budge, squirt some penetrating oil in at the point where the

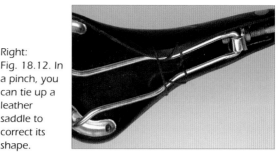

Left: Fig. 18.11. Details of a special clip to accept a double-wire leather saddle on a high-end seat post.

Right: Fig. 18.12. In a pinch, you can tie up a leather saddle to correct its shape.

seat lug is slotted, so it enters between the seatpost and the seat tube. Wait 2–3 minutes and try again. Pull the seatpost all the way out.

Installation procedure:

Do this *after* the saddle has been installed on the new seatpost.

1. Apply grease to the inside of the seat tube and the outside of the seatpost.

2. Insert the seatpost in the seat tube.

3. Move it to the exact location where you want it to be, but make sure the marker that shows the minimum insertion depth is not exposed.

4. Holding the saddle at the right height and straight ahead, tighten the binder bolt or the quick-release. (If the

quick-release can't be tightened properly, flip it to "open" again, adjust the thumb nut on the other side, and try again.)

5. Check to make sure the position is correct, and fine-tune the various adjustments, if necessary. You may find that you now need to adjust the angle and forward position in accordance with the applicable instructions above.

Note:

• At least 2½ inches (6.5 cm) of the seatpost must be clamped in. Usually the seatpost is marked to show this safe insertion depth.

Maintenance of Leather Saddle

A real leather saddle stretches with use, especially if it is allowed to get

wet. The best way to maintain its integrity is to treat the cover with leather grease (available from the saddle manufacturer, but any mineral oil or grease will do in a pinch; just don't use vegetable oil) once or twice a year. Let it sit overnight so it penetrates properly before using the seat. Occasionally, you may also have to tension the saddle cover to account for stretch.

Tools and equipment:

• special saddle wrench available from the saddle manufacturer (i.e., probably Brooks, the major surviving leather saddle manufacturer)

Procedure:

1. Look under the saddle cover near the tip (referred to as the "nose" of the saddle) and identify the bolt that holds the tip of the saddle cover to the wires, then find the

nut on this bolt for adjusting.

2. Tighten the nut by about ½ turn at a time until the saddle cover has the right tension. Do not overtighten.

Note:

If the saddle cover "sags," flaring out at the sides near the front, you can usually rescue it as follows:

1. Drill a series of four or five ³⁄₃₂-inch (2 mm) diameter holes about ¾ inch (20 mm) apart, about ½ inch (12 mm) above the lower edge on both sides of the flared out area.

2. Using a thin round shoe lace, tie the two sides together into an acceptable shape and tie the ends of the shoe lace together in a firm knot kept out of sight.

CHAPTER 19

Frame and Fork Maintenance

Although the frameset (i.e., the frame with the front fork) is the biggest of the bicycle's components, it's not really subject to the kind of damage that calls for repair and maintenance very much. The few things that can happen — and the even fewer things that can be done about them — are covered in this chapter.

The frame traditionally consists of steel tubing brazed or welded together into a roughly diamond-shaped structure. The frame itself comprises the main frame, built up from large diameter tubing, and the rear triangle made of smaller diameter tubing. The front fork is free to rotate in the main frame's head tube by means of the headset (see Chapter 17).

In recent years, frame construction and design have changed quite a bit, especially due to the use of different materials and the proliferation of suspension systems, especially on mountain bikes. As for materials, many frames are now made of aluminum alloys, while also titanium, carbon fiber, and magnesium are now in use.

The problem with all those "new" materials is that frames and forks made with them are even less repairable than steel frames are. The kind of damage that a frame or a fork is likely to sustain is either so minor that it doesn't really matter much (e.g., scratched paint) or so major that it can't be fixed, and requires replacement. Therefore this chapter mainly deals with checking for damage, rather than actually fixing things once they are damaged. The one thing you can do — at least on a frame made of steel or welded aluminum — is touching up the paint, and that will be covered at the end of the chapter.

Frame Inspection

After the bike has been in a fall or collision, check it over thoroughly. If there are signs of bending, buckling, or cracking, take it to a bike shop and ask what you should do.

The two most significant areas to watch out for are the front fork and

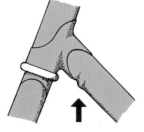

Fig. 19.2. Drawing of typical frame damage at the downtube resulting from frontal collision. Don't ride the bike if it's damaged this way.

Left: Fig. 19.1. Conventional high-end lugged and brazed frame. Many frames today are built up without lugs, which is cheaper.

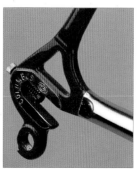

Fig. 19.3. Right-hand drop-out with wheel position adjusting screw and derailleur mounting eye.

the area of the down tube just behind the lower headset. If you see any bulging or cracking, check with the bike shop (whose advice is probably to discard the frame or the fork). If there is no obvious damage, check for distortion of frame and fork, as per the following procedures.

Frame Alignment Check

It's not safe to ride a bike with a frame that is misaligned, meaning that the front and rear wheels don't exactly follow one another in the same track. It negatively affects the balance of the bike, both when going straight and, even more unpredictably, when cornering. You can check

Fig. 19.4. Vertical dropout with derailleur eye.

the alignment of the frame yourself.

Tools and equipment:

- 10 feet (3 m) of twine
- calipers (or straight-edge with mm markings)

Procedure:

1. Wrap the twine around the frame from the right-hand rear dropout to the head tube, pull it around and run it back to the left-hand dropout.

2. Measure the distance between the twine and the frame's seat tube on the right and

Fig. 19.5. Front derailleurs on high-end road bikes are often mounted directly to this kind of lug brazed on to the frame's seat tube.

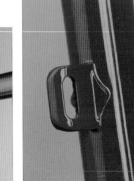

the left and record the results.

3. If the two measurements differ, the frame is misaligned — just how much is *too* much is up for debate, but I would say that any difference in excess of 3 mm ($1/8$ inch) is probably unsafe. At least take the bike to a bike shop and ask for advice.

Dropout Alignment Check

The dropouts (i.e., the flat plates on which the rear wheel is installed) should be parallel for the wheel to align properly.

Tools and equipment:

- 18-inch (45 cm) metal straightedge
- calipers

Right:
Fig. 19.6.
Frame
alignment
check.

Procedure

1. Hold the metal straightedge perpendicular to one of the dropouts, extending in the direction of the seat tube and measure the distance between ruler and seat tube.

2. Do the same on the other dropout.

3. Compare the measurements. Again, there is some latitude for interpretation as to what constitutes unsafe misalignment, but I'd ask for professional advice at a bike shop if the difference is more than 3 mm ($1/8$ inch).

Fork Inspection

What matters here is the alignment of the two fork blades relative to each other and relative to the steerer tube. On a regu-

lar fork, you can usually check the alignment by means of a visual inspection.

Tools and equipment:

- calipers
- flat, level surface

Procedure:

1. Place the fork flat on the level surface, supporting it at the fork crown and the upper straight section of the fork blades.

2. Compare the distance between the level surface and the fork ends. If there's a difference, they're misaligned.

3. Visually establish whether the line that goes through the center of the steerer tube also goes through the center of the upper straight portion of the fork blades. If it doesn't, you have misalignment between the fork blades and the steerer tube.

4. Also in this case, once you have established that there is misalignment, go to a bike shop and get advice on what to do.

Front Fork Installation

To turn a loose frame and a separate fork into a frameset, you have to install the front fork in the frame. Most of the work involved is referenced in Chapter 17, which covers the headset, because the headset is the link between the frame and the fork.

First make sure that the headset fits both the fork's steerer tube and the frame's head tube. Not only is there the difference between threaded and threadless steerer tubes, depending on the type of headset used, there are also steerer tubes and headsets in different diameters.

Also the length of the steerer tube must add up to the height of the frame's head tube plus the "stacking height" of the headset (and the stem height plus any spacers in the case of a threadless headset).

Additionally, there's the distinction between regular forks and suspension forks. If you are trying to install a suspension fork in a frame not specifically designed for one, explain that at the bike shop before buying the fork, because for safe handling, you should avoid altering the bike's steering geometry too much.

For all other details, see the installation procedure in Chapter 17 in the overhauling instructions for the particular type of headset used.

Paint Touch-Up

When a regular painted, brazed or welded metal frame or fork shows any scratches, you can touch up the paint to prevent rust and to keep the bike looking as nice as possible. Don't do this on carbon fiber frames, nor on a frame with bonded joints (as opposed to one that's brazed or welded), because the solvents used either in preparation or actual painting may weaken the epoxy, possible voiding the warranty.

Fig. 19.7. Measuring the distance between the frame's seat tube and the twine for the frame alignment check.

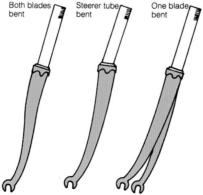

Fig. 19.8. Drawing of typical fork damage.

129

Fig. 19.9. Paint touch-up.

Tools and equipment:

• matching paint (if not available from the manufacturer, buy a close match in a model shop)

• tiny brush

• steel wool or emery cloth

• paint thinner

• cloth

Procedure:

1. Thoroughly clean the area of (and around) the damage.

2. Use emery cloth or a tiny spec of steel wool to remove corrosion, dirt, and paint remnants down to the bare, shiny metal surface in the damaged spot.

3. Clean the spot to be repainted once more with a cloth soaked in paint thinner, and wipe it dry.

4. Shake the paint thoroughly to mix it well.

5. Using the tiny brush, just barely dipped in paint, apply paint only to the damaged area.

6. Let dry at least 24 hours, and repeat steps 4 and 5, if necessary.

CHAPTER 20

Suspension Maintenance

Since the early 1990s, there has been a trend toward the integration of suspension systems on bicycles. Not only downhill mountain bikes, where many modern systems were first used, but even commuter bicycles often come with some form of suspension these days.

Sometimes this means no more than replacing a standard fork or seat post by a sprung version of essentially the same item, without much change to the rest of the bike. However, in other cases, it means that the bicycle is designed specifically around a suspension system, giving it an entirely different look.

Suspension Forks

Most common are telescoping suspension forks, suitable for installation on an otherwise "normal" bike. These forks incorporate two sets of tubes that slide inside each other, the inner ones (the stanchion tubes) being guided in the outer ones (called slider tubes) and connected with spring elements. The spring elements are either elastomer pads, metal spiral springs, or air cartridges, and different types may be combined on different sides of the same fork.

By way of preventive maintenance, the most important thing is to regularly is to clean the stanchion tubes, wiping away from the point where they enter the slider tubes (after each use in wet weather or dirty terrain).

In addition, check the suspension fork once

Above: Fig. 20.4. Adjusting points at the bottom of a high-end suspension fork.

Below: Fig. 20.5. They've almost disappeared with the advent of cheap suspension forks, but this is how you adjust a suspension stem.

Fig. 20.1. Typical modern telescopic suspension fork.

Fig. 20.2. Complicated forks like these, with many pivot points, are more susceptible to wear and damage.

Fig. 20.3. Adjusting the preload on a telescopic suspension fork.

a season to make sure it is working properly, proceeding as follows:

Suspension Fork Check

Tools and equipment:

- Usually none required

Procedure:

1. Holding the bike firmly at the headset, try to wiggle the bottom of the fork at the fork-ends. If they move loosely, you have a problem, which you should refer to a bike shop mechanic.

2. Holding the bike from the front at the

handlebars, push down with all your body weight and observe how the suspension fork reacts. If all is well, it goes down with increasing resistance but does not stop suddenly.

3. With the suspension fork pushed in as in Step 2, release pressure and observe whether the recovery is smooth and quick.

4. If any of the criteria above are not met, you may have a problem, and it's recommended you refer it to a bike shop.

Fig. 20.6. Simple solution for those who like an upright riding posture: suspension seat post.

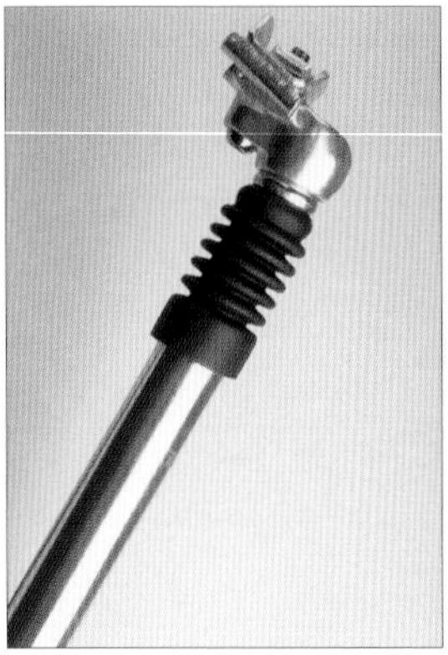

Suspension Fork Maintenance

For this work, refer to the instruction manual that came with the specific fork. In addition to cleaning, as described above, you may be able to adjust one or more of the following:

- preload, which controls the response rate, i.e., how easy it is to compress the fork

- damping, i.e., how much it sea-saws after compression and release

- travel, i.e., by how many cm the fork can go down and back up again)

- rebound rate, i.e., how quickly it recovers after compression

On different forks, there may be different methods and locations for making these adjustments, mainly depend-

Fig. 20.7. Preload adjustment on a suspension seat post. Don't unscrew the plug to the point where it does not fully engage the screw thread.

ing on the type of spring elements used.

Suspension Seatposts

These items are used to help smooth the ride on bikes intended for an upright rider position (e.g., city bikes), but without "real" rear suspension. (In fact, never use a suspension seat post on a bike with rear suspension because the effect of the two suspension methods against each other may ruin the more sophisticated rear suspension element.)

Preload is the only factor that can be adjusted on the suspension seat post. To do that, remove the seat post from the bike, as described in Chapter 18, and use an Allan wrench to tighten or loosen the preload adjuster plug in the bottom of the seat post — turning it in tightens the

Right:
Fig. 20.8.
The working parts of a suspension seat post.

Left: Fig. 20.9. One of many possibilities for rear suspension, pivoted just behind the bottom bracket.

Right: Fig. 20.10. Another solution, pivoted at the same point but a more complex rear structure — and more pivot points, leading to more potential wear.

Fig. 20.11. This type of rear suspension, pivoted in front of and above the bottom bracket, is referred to as "sweet spot."

initial compression of the spring element inside; turning it out slackens it. For the sake of safety, don't unscrew it so far that any part of the adjuster plug extends from the seat post end (at least the beginning of the internal screw threads in the seat post must be visible).

If you want to install a suspension seat post on a bike that did not originally come with one, make sure you get one of the same diameter, measured in mm, as the original seat post (use calipers to measure the diameter if it is not marked on the seat post). Of course, it must also be clamped in far enough, but that's rarely a problem because these things are awfully long

— in fact, they're only suitable if your frame is quite small for you.

Rear Suspension

There are many different methods used to achieve rear suspension on a bicycle. Unfortunately, the more sophisticated, the more troublesome the rear suspension is likely to be. Those sophisticated ones, e.g., the ones used on downhill mountain bikes, tend to have many linkages and pivot points, which all add up to potential loose connections, due to wear after some use.

From a maintenance standpoint, there are just two things to watch, and they're common on all those different types: the suspension element itself and the pivot points where the different linkage elements rotate relative to the frame or relative to each other.

Keep all these parts clean, and lightly lubricate the pivot points regularly, using a nongreasy lubricant, such as a wax-based one, or even WD-40. Wipe off any excess lubricant. Also tighten the pivot bolts once a month.

CHAPTER 21

Accessory Maintenance

An accessory, as opposed to a component, is defined as any part that is, or can be, installed on the bike but is not part of its essential operation. Thus, brakes are not accessories, but bells and whistles are — except where the law prescribes that a bicycle must be equipped with a bell.

Literally hundreds of accessories have been introduced for bicycle use at different times. What they all have in common is some kind of attachment to the bike. And that's indeed the most common maintenance aspect of all components. In addition, there will be some more specific advice concerning the most important and/or common accessories in use today:

- lock
- pump
- lights and reflectors
- bicycle computer
- luggage racks
- fenders
- kick stand

General Accessory Comments

The two tenets of accessory maintenance are:

- keep it tightly mounted
- replace (or remove) it if it's broken

The last thing you want on the bike is an accessory that hangs loose or doesn't even do its job. Check the installation hardware regularly, tightening all nuts, bolts, and clamps. And by all means, remove the item if it doesn't work and you haven't been able to fix it. Before replacing it in that case, ask yourself whether you could do without it altogether, and don't replace it if you could.

Fig. 21.1. About as much as you're likely to see on a bike in the US: a rack and a bag.

Fig. 21.2. The fully accessorized bicycle has been developed into an art form in places like the Netherlands, where I picked up this one. It has all the accessories to make the bicycle practical as a means of everyday transportation.

Fig. 21.3. Most importantly, regularly check the attachment of all accessories.

Generally, any attachment hardware should have at least two mounting bolts, so vibration is less likely to rattle it loose. Another thing to watch out for is that items clamped around another part of the bike should fit snugly — and

preferably there should be a flexible plastic or rubber protective sleeve around the bicycle component first, which helps protect the bike's finish and aids in keeping the accessory mounting hardware in place.

Lock

There's not much maintenance required on this, unfortunately, most essential accessory. Lubrication is done once or twice a year by inserting the nozzle of a thin lubricant, such as WD-40, at the point where the bolt enters into the lock mechanism and spraying in just a tiny little

squirt of oil. In addition, you can put some oil on the key, insert it in the lock, and then close and open the lock 2 or 3 times to lubricate it. If your lock can be attached to the bike frame, check and tighten the bolt or the clamp that holds it during the monthly inspection.

Pump

I suggest you use two kinds of pumps: a floor pump for at home and a frame-mounted hand pump for on the road. Once or twice a year, tighten the screw cap at the head. If the pump doesn't work, first take

the head apart, and you may have to replace the thick flexible grommet.

The other item that sometimes gives trouble is the rubber or plastic plunger inside the barrel. It can be reached by unscrewing the cap at the point where the plunger mechanism enters the barrel. Flex it, knead it, apply some lubricant to

Above: Fig. 21.4. To lubricate a lock, spray a little oil on the key (shown here) and the bolt, then open and close it a few times.

Below: Fig. 21.5. Not bomb-proof, but convenient: integral lock attached to the frame.

Top left: Fig. 21.6. The trend in pumps these days is small. Actually, longer pumps generally work better.

Bottom left: Fig. 21.7. The guts of the small pump shown above.

Above: Fig. 21.8. The grommet that holds the valve. This pump has a lever to clamp it firmly in place on the valve.

Below: Fig. 21.9. Simple battery light using four AA-cells.

135

it, and if you can't get it to work, you'll probably have to replace the pump unless you can find a replacement.

Lights

Perhaps the most important accessories for the rider's safety, bicycle lights are also the most significantly improved since the early 1980s. Today, excellent lighting systems and individual lights, both front and rear, are readily available at most bike shops. There are three general types of bicycle lights in use today:

- battery lights with dry cell batteries in the light unit
- battery lights with separate, central battery
- generator (dynamo) lights

Battery lights with built-in batteries

In the front, these usually clamp directly or indirectly to the handlebars, or in England often to a clip on the fork. In the rear, they attach either to the seat post or e.g., to a luggage rack or the seat stays. The one used for the front should be bright and produce a compact bundle of light that should be aimed at an area of the road

about 20–30 feet (6–9 m) in front of the bike. Usually, there's a clamp that stays on the handlebars once installed and the light just slides and clips into this clamp, so you can remove it when you leave the bike unguarded.

The one for the rear should be red, and point straight back (neither up nor down, neither left nor right). The rear light does not need to be quite so bright as the one in front. LEDs appear to be very suitable for this use, mainly because they provide much longer battery life. The LEDs themselves also last much longer than light bulbs — however, they don't last forever ei-

ther, and the light will have to be replaced if they become dim.

The most common maintenance required on battery lights is replacing the batteries and the bulbs. A battery charge typically lasts less than 4 hours, so it's a good idea to carry spares (and especially if you use rechargeable ones, recharge them at least once a month). Before you go on a longer ride that may take you in the evening, check the condition of both the batteries in the light and the spare batteries.

If you use rechargeable batteries, note the difference between the two most common types

Fig. 21.10. More sophisticated are lights with a central battery. However, all the wiring and connections make them more susceptible to damage.

Fig. 21.11. Headlight for generator lighting unit. Occasionally check the bracket for cracks, because it tends to break due to vibrations.

Fig. 21.12. Generator light with the headlight mounted to the same bracket on the front fork. Actually, for the generator, the rear wheel would be a safer place.

Fig. 21.13. The bottom bracket generator is mounted against the rear wheel, directly behind the bottom bracket. Problem: this is a messy location and it may slip in wet weather.

of lights. Since the lights are designed for standard-size cells, only NiCad (Nickel-Cadmium) and NiMH (Nickel-Metal-Hydride) are available: the NiMH batteries last considerably longer but are much more expensive. However, since they also have a longer shelf life (i.e., they will hold a charge when not used much longer), they're worth the extra.

Bulbs typically don't last more than about

100 hours of use. Get some spare bulbs and carry one for each light on the bike, e.g., in the tire patch kit. If you use the nice bright halogen bulbs, don't touch the glass with your bare hands, because the acidity will etch the glass dull, reducing their light output once they get hot.

Lights with central battery

These lights are typically more powerful and often have high beam and low beam capabilities. Their larger battery, consisting of several cells wired up together, are either packaged in a pouch tied to the bike or neatly packed away in something that fits in a water bottle cage (actually, a real water bottle is often used, with the battery cells inserted and the space around them filled with some kind of compound to keep everything in place).

Again, the batteries and the bulbs need to be checked and replaced, if necessary (although the batteries are almost al-

ways rechargeable, in which case you just plug the unit in via its recharging adapter, which should do the trick in about 2 hours). In addition to NiCad and NiMH batteries, there are also lead-acid gel batteries. The latter require different care: they have to be recharged *before* they are fully discharged, i.e., before the light gets dim, whereas the other types seem to last longest if they are drained completely before they are recharged. See the preceding section *Battery lights with built-in battery* for more information regarding spare bulbs and batteries.

In addition to bulbs and batteries, there is

Fig. 21.14. Replacing the light bulb. Don't touch halogen bulbs with your bare fingers.

Fig. 21.15. Battery-powered LED rear light strapped to the seat post.

Left:
Fig. 21.16. Battery-powered LED rear light with clamp to attach to the seat stays.

Fig. 21.17. The guts of a battery-powered LED rear light exposed. In flashing mode, batteries will last at least 100 hours (much less when burning constantly) — and it's more visible in flashing mode.

Fig. 21.18. Separate rear light and reflector mounted on the rear fender and the luggage rack, respectively, on a Dutch city bike.

wiring to deal with. So, if the light doesn't work and you've checked the bulb and the battery, and found them to be OK, check the wiring. Usually it's a connection at the end of the wiring, so check there first and fix it with a soldering iron and solder. If there are any exposed metal wire parts, use electrical insu-

Above: Fig. 21.19. Typical bicycle computer.

Below: Fig. 21.20. The computer is mounted by means of a clip that stays on the bike. Keep the electrical contacts on these two parts free from dirt and corrosion.

lating tape to fix it. You may have to replace the wiring completely if you can't identify the source of the problem.

Generator lights

This type also has a central power source and wiring connecting it to the light — actually it usually feeds both a front light and a rear light. Usually, the electricity is carried by a single wire and returned to the generator via the metal of the bike, for which purpose each part — generator, front light, and rear light — has a pinch-screw to make what's called a mass contact.

The safest place for the generator is on the rear wheel, where accidental loosening does not impose the risk of a serious accident as much as it does in the front. Even so, keep it tightened property. It

should be mounted so that the longitudinal centerline points to the center of the hub.

Here too, the most common problem, other than burned-out bulbs, is wiring failure. Especially the point where the wires connect to the dynamo is subject to accidental disconnection. Check it frequently and be careful to route your wire in such a way that it isn't likely to get caught when e.g., storing or parking the bike.

There are also two generator-specific problems: slip and mass connections. To prevent slip, which is most common in wet weather, make sure it is mounted in such a way that it runs on a smooth or lightly ribbed rubber part of the tire, rather than the almost uncovered sidewall of a skinny tire on the one hand or the thick knobbies on a mountain bike tire on the other. If

Left: Fig. 21.21. Luggage rack installation detail at the seat stays.

it still slips, try to increase the pressure with which the spring pushes it against the tire by bending in the mounting bracket (do that with the generator in the disengaged position).

Above: Fig. 21.22. Luggage rack installation detail at the rear drop-outs.

Below: Fig. 21.23. Luggage rack and fenders on a modern hybrid city bike.

Reflectors

Like lights, these are safety items, and you really need them in the dark (not just at night: they're just as essential e.g., in a tunnel). Make sure they're mounted firmly and point straight back (for the one in the rear) and forward (for the

Fig. 21.24 (above) and Fig, 21.25 (below): Luggage rack and fender attachment details on a city bike. In the front, you'd be better off with an attachment that can break loose under moderate force.

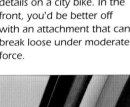

one in the front). Although the one in the back can give adequate protection, never solely rely on the one on front — get a front light, which is more visible over a wider angle of coverage for all directions from which you may be endangered *and* allows you to see where you're going yourself.

Replace any reflector that is cracked or broken, because water can enter through the crack and "fog up" the reflective pattern on the inside of the lense.

Bicycle Computer

Bicycle computers have also improved dramatically over time. Even so, they're still fidgety items.

Fig. 21.26. Mud flap to keep the rain off your shoes.

Check the installation of the pickup and the matching sensor, to make sure they pass each other closely. Check the condition of the wire, and tie it down at intermediate points with zip-ties or electric insulating tape so they don't get caught or damaged. And again, if it doesn't work, replace or discard the entire system, computer, mounting bracket, sensor, pick-up, wire, and all.

Luggage Rack

Luggage racks, or carriers, are available both for the front and the rear. Although the rear is the most common place for heavy and bulky items, a well-mounted front rack can help stabilize the bike if it has to be heavily loaded. For the installation of racks, it's preferable if the frame and the front fork have brazed-on

Right:
Fig. 21.27.
Fully enclosed chain guard on a Dutch city bike. Unclipping the back portion gives access to the cog.

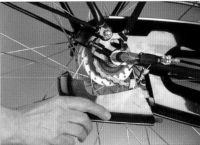

bosses and eyelets at the dropouts and fork ends to attach the rack to.

If there are no bosses, you can install clips around the fork and the stays (providing it's not a super lightweight bike). However, especially at the fork, which has tapered fork blades (thicker at the top, tapering to thinner near the bottom), there is a risk of the clips slipping. Mount a rubber or flexible plastic sleeve between the clip and the bike, and frequently check the connections (daily on a loaded tour), tightening them firmly.

Fenders

Both during and after rainfall, fenders (mud guards) help keep water and mud off the bike, its rider, and those following. Again, make sure they're firmly connected at the various mounting

Fig. 21.28.
Kick stand mounting by
means of large Allan bolt.

Fig. 21.29.
Kick stand mounting on
low-end bike.

flap, and attach the flap
to the mudguard with a
set of 4 mm bolts, nuts,
and washers.

Kick Stand

Also called prop stand,
this device is found
mainly on low-end bikes.
On a frame that's prop-
erly designed for its use,
it can be an OK item,
because there's a flat
plate to which it is bolted
with either a 10 mm
Allan bolt or a regular
hexagonal bolt.

   If the frame was not
designed for installation
of a kick stand, it is
usually clamped around
the chain stays just for-
ward of the bridge piece
that connects them. My
advice is to remove it,
because it tends to
come loose, twist
around, and damage the
chainstay. However, if
you must have one on
your bike, at least tighten
it once a month — or try
to find the type that is
clamped on at the rear
wheel axle.

Fig. 21.30. Most modern
bells don't have a
mechanism inside, so don't
need maintenance. If it does
have a mechanism, give it a
drop of oil once a month.

Warning Devices

Either a bell, a horn, or a
whistle will alert others to
your presence, but only
the first will identify you
as a cyclist. That may be
a disadvantage (e.g,
when dealing with cal-
lous fellow-travelers) or
an advantage (to those
who understand the cy-
clist's predicament). As
for installation and maintenance of a bell, mount
it within easy reach and
keep the mounting bolt
tight. If there's a metal
mechanism inside, give
it a drop of oil from time
to time.

points. Also check to
make sure they don't rub
against the tire or an-
other moving part.

   If the fenders and
their mounting hardware
are not very rigid (and almost none of the avail-
able ones sold as after-
market accessories are
very rigid), at least the
one in the front should
have a clip that will come
loose if the fender gets
caught in the wheel, so
as to prevent a serious
accident due to the front
wheel locking up. Just
the same, check the
connections regularly
and tighten the hardware

— or discard the fender
if you can't get it tight
enough.

   At the bottom of the
front fender, it's a good
idea to install a flexible
mud flap, which keeps
splashing water off your
feet and the lower part of
the bike. Since they are
rarely available in US
bike shops, you can
make one yourself from
any flexible material,
whether it's a piece cut
off a discarded water
bottle or a piece of the
uppers of an old rubber
boot. Drill 5 mm holes in
the bottom of the fender
and in the top of the

Bibliography

Baird, Stewart. *Performance Cycling: The Scientific Way to Get the Most out of Your Bicycle.* San Francisco: Van der Plas Publications, 2000.

Ballantine, Richard. *Richard's 21st-Century Bicycle Book.* Woodstock, NY: Overlook Press, 2001.

Barnett, John. *Barnett's Manual: Analysis and Procedures for Bike Mechanics.* 4th. Ed. Boulder, CO: VeloPress, 2001.

Berto, Frank, R. Shepherd, R. Henry. *The Dancing Chain: History and Development of the Derailleur Bicycle.* San Francisco: Van der Plas Publications, 2000.

Berto, Frank. *Bicycling Magazine's Complete Guide to Upgrading Your Bicycle.* Emmaus, PA: Rodale Press, 1989.

Bicycling Magazine's Complete Guide to Bicycle Maintenance and Repair. Emmaus, PA: Rodale Press, 1994.

Brandt, Jobst. *The Bicycle Wheel.* 3rd. Ed. Palo Alto: Avocet, 1995.

Burrows, Mike. *Bicycle Design: Towards the Perfect Machine.* York (GB): Open Road / Seattle: Alpenbooks, 2000.

Cole, Clarence, H. J. Glenn, John S. Allen. *Glenn's New Complete Bicycle Manual.* New York: Crown Publishers, 1987.

Cuthberson, Tom. *Anybody's Bike Book.* Berkeley, CA: Ten-Speed Press, 1998.

DeLong, Fred: *DeLong's Guide to Bicycles and Bicycling: The Art and Science.* 2nd Edn. Radnor (PA): Chilton Books, 1978.

Ries, Richard. *Building Your Perfect Bike: From Bare Frame to Personalized Superbike.* Osceola, WI: MBI Publishing, 1997.

Sutherland, Howard. *Sutherland's Handbook for Bicycle Mechanics.* 4th Edn. Berkeley: Sutherland Publications, 2000.

Van der Plas, Rob. *The Bicycle Repair Book.* 2nd Edn. San Francisco: Bicycle Books, 1993.

——. *Bicycle Technology: Understanding, Selecting, and Maintaining the Modern Bicycle and its Components.* San Francisco: Bicycle Books, 1991.

——. *Buying a Bike: How to Get the Best Bike for Your Money.* San Francisco: Van der Plas Publications, 1999.

——. *Mountain Bike Maintenance.* 4th Edn. Osceola, WI: MBI Publishing, 2002.

——. *Road Bike Maintenance: Repairing and Maintaining the Modern Lightweight Bicycle.* San Francisco: Bicycle Books, 1996.

Zinn, Lennard. *Zinn and the Art of Mountain Bike Repair.* Boulder, CO: 1995.

——. *Mountain Bike Performance Handbook.* Osceola, WI: MBI Publishing / Boulder, CO: VeloPress, 1998.

——. *Zinn and the Art of Road Bike Maintenance.* Boulder, CO: VeloPress, 2000.

Index